Jan Johnson writes with beautiful transparency, inviting us to journey alongside her as she tenderly reminisces about her personal moments of grief. This book is sure to ease hurting hearts and encourage those navigating seasons of deep ꞏꞏꞏ s. With an incredible ability to lean ꞏ of life's most painful hardships, Jan ꞏ-filled wisdom—beyond the pain. l here," Jan's comforting relatability ꞏ onger, joyful tomorrows.

—**LaTan Roland Murphy**, author of *Courageous Women of The Bible*

Janet K. Johnson has written a heartfelt devotional to help guide you through your own grief process. This devotional shares the author's experiences through life and how she saw the Lord's hand in her every day experiences. As a marriage and family therapist who works with clients with PTSD and trauma, I can share that this devotional has touched me deeply. I have found it completely comforting for me to remember that the Lord is always with us. This is a lovely book to help those who are on their own journey of grief.

—**Amanda Booth Bice**, MA, marriage and family therapist, Heart of the Matter Counseling

Tragedy, loss, and grief are no strangers to Janet. She leads her readers by example in how to walk the path of sorrow and still experience peace, knowing that we are not alone in our journey and there is hope. This beautiful work is anchored in the truth that somehow, beyond our understanding, God will use the worst of circumstances for our good."

—**Lori Heagney**, professional counselor, Summit Wellness Centers

Grief: The Unwanted Journey is an inspiring and well-crafted book, a "thirst-quenching" journey that will satisfy readers by helping them to understand and process their own grief. This book is a deep well for the journey we all have or will experience. It is based on Scripture with wonderful "God Moments" and is a must read for all brothers and sisters in Christ.

—**James Bice**, Major, USAF retired, Stephens Minister, and Life Coach

GRIEF
the Unwanted
Journey

May these reflections bring
nourishment to your soul.
Joyfully in Christ,
Janet

GRIEF

the Unwanted
Journey

Reflections to Help Navigate Your Way
through Tragedy and Loss

JANET K. JOHNSON

To my Lord and Savior, Jesus Christ, who has not only traveled with me through times of sorrow and joy but has gone ahead to prepare for my final homecoming.

To my family, who has been a source of support, encouragement, and love during times of joy and sorrow, as well as during my times of learning to trust and never give up. Rick, Mark, David, James, and Rebecca, thank you.

To the saints mentioned in this book whose lives forever touched mine and which I now share through the stories from my memories.

My brother Ken
My father and mother
Our son David
My friends Debbie and Linda
My father-in-law and mother-in-law
My brother-in-law Ron

Contents

Season Three
Anger Delays Me Reaching My Destination

Season Four
Unpredictable Emotions Take Me On Many Detours

Season Five
Depression Causes Me to Go Back

Season Six
Forgiveness Helps Me Breathe Fresh Air Along the Way

Season Seven
Acceptance Helps Me See the Clouds Moving On

Season Eight
Hope and a New Normal Show Me the Path More Clearly

Introduction

Have you ever read *Alexander and the Terrible, Horrible, No Good, Very Bad Day* by Judith Viorst? If your days don't seem to be all they should, it might just help. I don't want to spoil it for those of you who haven't read it, but let's just say that Alexander gets gum in his hair, has trouble at school, falls in the mud, gets soap in his eyes, bites his tongue, feels as though no one listens to him, and decides it would be better to move to some far-off place. There have been days—many days, in fact—when I haven't even wanted to get out of bed. At least Alexander did that!

I heard a statement one time that reminded me not only of Alexander's days but also about the many ups-and-downs I have faced in my life. Even as I have written the reflections for this book, I have relived some of the moments that caught me by surprise—and not in a good way. Tragedy and loss have touched my life, just as they probably have yours. To live is to experience loss. These losses may come from the deaths of loved ones or having to move away from those you hold dear. Sometimes loss comes by way of a divorce, financial reversal, termination of a job, or having to let go of future hopes and dreams. There are those who encounter loss because of aging or health issues. So many mornings we get up to find that the day feels hopeless and, if it didn't start like that, it certainly might end that way.

The statement I referred to went like this: "God promised that everything will be okay in the end. So, if everything is not okay, then this is not the end."

Well, if everything is going to be okay, then maybe there is hope for each day!

My prayer is that the reflections in this book will help you in the struggles you face as you journey through loss and grief. Whether you use the reflections in order or by topic, based on how you are feeling on any particular day, makes no difference. Grief is a journey, and each person's journey in grief is different. Give yourself grace and time for the process. Invite God into each day and know that you do not face any day alone.

On really bad days I have discovered that it helps to return to a place in my mind that brought me a sense of peace and hope. For me that was as a girl, wading in a clear, gently flowing stream. Notice I said stream, not raging river. For me, there was something about being in the gurgling water that was refreshing. Like the currents of water that flowed around the protruding rocks, my way around them became obvious due to the currents. Those memories remind me that there are safe ways around the rocks (life's tragedies and losses) that appear and that, even if I fall, it is possible to pick myself up again and keep on wading.

As I look back, there have been many rocks I have had to navigate on my journey thus far. As a young girl I always felt that I wasn't quite good enough. I knew my parents loved me, but I always thought that if I got better at whatever I did, they might love me more. As a teenager I was attacked on the way home from school—an experience that replaced my trust with fear. Later, in college, I faced classes that challenged my faith and my ability to continually do better, and as the result of graduations, I experienced inevitable separations from others I cherished. As a military wife, that scenario replayed itself over and over. Either people were leaving before we left, or we moved away.

The crushing tragedies, however, began when one of our sons turned out to be what James Dobson labels a "strong-willed child." He became our prodigal. This child, who was loved deeply, created disunity and heartache in our family. It took years and much love to help him understand how deeply that love went.

Then there was my brother, my only sibling, who was murdered. There are no words to describe the depth of that pain. That was followed by my father's lingering death from cancer. Years later, our prodigal returned home and was killed in an accident—eight months after he was married and just when it looked as though his life was beginning to shine. After personally struggling to make sense of all that had happened to that point, my mother joined other loved ones who had gone before her to their eternal home.

Amid these losses came the death of a mother-in-law, whose surgery was intended to bring her new energy and life but instead ended her life. She was later joined in eternity by my father-in-law, whose journey through Alzheimer's stripped him of his life. Then one day we learned that my brother-in-law had committed suicide, leaving two children and several grandchildren.

I have not mentioned a very close college friend who died much too young, a prayer sister and best friend who suffered a stroke and, though still living, has continued to experience lingering side effects. There are others. We can all identify with many losses. These are mine.

What I have learned through all these tragedies and losses is that God has been there. I couldn't always see Him or feel Him, but I've been assured of His presence because I know He holds me so closely that He catches my tears (Psalm 56:8). Not only has He been there, but God has been the stream into which I have wandered for the refreshing of my soul. Seeking His comfort and strength has allowed me to know that, in the end, all will be okay.

Perhaps that calls for bold print: **in the end, it will be okay.** That is God's great promise for those who love Jesus as their Savior. The end will be better than okay, because Jesus has overcome all our earthly struggles, and has a place for each one of us that far surpasses anything we can imagine.

And I heard a loud voice from the throne saying, "Look! God's dwelling place is now among the people, and he will dwell with them. They will be his people, and God himself will be with them and be their God. He will wipe every tear from their eyes. There will be no more death or mourning or crying or pain, for the old order of things has passed away."
(Revelation 21:3–4)

Season One

Tragedy Begins My Unwanted Journey

Life After Death? Yes!

Once too frail to do anything for herself, she now sat up without any help. Her arms, which had been so weak she had not been able to use them, were now raised outward from her body and upward toward heaven as though she were reaching for something—or Someone. Her eyes, which had been dim and steel gray, now had a twinkle, as though she were seeing something she had anticipated for a long time. In an instant my mother had gone from someone who seemed lifeless lying in bed to someone sitting up with an expression of anticipation and total peace.

My mother's death, which came moments later, offered me the gift of watching a deeply spiritual woman transition from her earthly life to her heavenly home. It was a moment in time when my understanding of life after death took on a meaning I had never truly grasped before. While I could not see what my mother saw, I knew she was seeing things in the heavenly realm and was being welcomed home. Even at her death, I beheld life.

As Christians, each year we celebrate the resurrection of Jesus. The Scriptures reveal that Jesus talked and walked, taught and encouraged His disciples *after* He had defeated death. He was, without question, alive!

While losing loved ones is never easy, the knowledge that they are experiencing life beyond this earthly world can bring incalculable comfort. We can trust in the power of the resurrection and know that the one(s) we grieve are now whole and at peace, experiencing joy beyond measure.

Sometimes, in *our* pain, it is difficult for us to be happy for the one who has gone before us to life eternal. Living without the physical presence of someone can be agonizingly hard. But recognizing that the great cloud of witnesses (including our loved ones if they knew Jesus as Lord) are pulling for us to be comforted and at peace can help us live more fully, even while we grieve.

I can only imagine my mother saw Jesus, and other departed loved ones, among the great cloud of witnesses that welcomed her as she transitioned from this earthly life. What I do *not* need to imagine is that *there is life beyond death!* That is the eternal promise to which you and I may cling.

Now faith is confidence in what we hope for and assurance about what we do not see.
(Hebrews 11:1)

God's Forever Promise

It was a Tuesday—Tuesday, September 16, 1975. Within me was a new life about to be born! I was in labor with our second son, David, who arrived in the afternoon and weighed in at 9 pounds, 13 ounces. As I held him in my arms, counted his tiny fingers and toes, and felt his full head of dark hair, I sensed a wonderful joy. I just wanted to hold him close.

Twenty-six years later our precious David was involved in an accident that he did not survive. When we received the call no parent ever wants to receive, memories of his impish grin, his ability to debate almost any issue, his love of fishing and the outdoors—and his love of family flooded my shattered heart. The depth of a parent's agony at losing a child for which she has cherished hopes and dreams cannot be measured or put into words. David's accident could not be explained. We will never know its cause. The pieces of my heart that were torn apart that day have mended, but the scars of the loss will always be present. While I can no longer hold him close, his life has touched mine forever.

Sudden, unexpected death has a life all its own. Often, conversations are left unfinished. A final word of love may go unspoken. Dreams of the future for the one who has died are left unaccomplished. Questions go unanswered.

In times like this we cannot have all the answers—nor do I think we are supposed to. That's where our faith takes over and we trust. Scripture tells us that in our eternal home there will be no more sadness or pain because death has been overcome by victory through Jesus Christ (1 Corinthians 15:54; Revelation 21:4). I am forever thankful for Jesus, who died for David. Even as David was being resuscitated in the helicopter on the way to the hospital, Jesus was preparing to receive him into his forever home, where one day I will hold him close again. That is God's promise.

> *"But your dead will live, Lord;*
> *their bodies will rise—*
> *let those who dwell in the dust*
> *wake up and shout for joy."*
> (Isaiah 26:19a)

A Moment in Time

Flash! A moment in time has been captured by the camera. The image it produces can be remembered forever just by a glance at the picture. In movies this is known as a flash frame. In life it is known as a defining moment—a time when life as we knew it was forever changed. We've all had them—those defining moments—those times when life stood still, and we were forever changed.

Our family had moved from Alaska, and we were taking a trip to Disney World. The advertisements in Alaska enticed our four children to expect this to be *the trip* of all trips. We were joined by long-time friends and their children, and all faced the day with anticipation. As we stood in the ticket line, the excitement of the children was palpable.

Just as we got through the gate and stood taking in the myriad of sights and sounds before us, over the loud speaker someone announced my name. I was instructed to find a phone and call the Disneyland operator. Then it happened. That moment in time that is forever etched in my mind. My mother's voice relayed that my only sibling, my brother Ken, had been murdered.

Murdered. The word pierced my heart. It took my breath away. I heard the words my mother spoke, but they were so unbelievable, so unexpected. Life has a way of throwing curveballs at us; it is not always fair. When we are faced by such a sudden death of a loved one, what do we do?

In the Gospel of John, chapter 11, a man named Lazarus became sick and died. He was a dear brother of Mary and Martha. The three were such close friends of Jesus that *Jesus wept.* Even Jesus cried when emotions became too overwhelming to handle. He saw His friends hurting; He witnessed their desperation and felt their pain. Amid our pain and sorrow over earthly death, Jesus stands with us sharing our grief.

Those moments in time will always be remembered. As God heals our grief, there will be other moments that bring smiles as we remember how precious those loved ones were. God's Spirit within us grieves, even as He rejoices with us as we exchange the tragedy for the triumph of eternal life. What God has for us, as we create our new flash frame with our loved one in heaven, has more power than any bullet or knife or drug. Praise God for making all things new!

"So, do not fear, for I am with you;
do not be dismayed, for I am your God.
I will strengthen you and help you;
I will uphold you with my righteous right hand."
(Isaiah 41:10)

Out of the Sky

From Buffalo to Chicago and on to Evansville, Indiana. I had made the flight many times during my college career and knew what to expect. Somewhere between Chicago and Indianapolis, however, my eyes caught sight of something unusual—flames shooting from the turbo prop engine. My adrenaline increased, knowing this was not usual. Others had noticed it as well; I saw fingers pointing toward the fire. Passengers questioning the flight attendant were told that the captain was aware, but she then abruptly headed toward the cockpit. Feelings of helplessness and fear pervaded my entire being. Suddenly, a big puff of black smoke bellowed from the engine, and it was unmistakable there was a problem. Passengers tightened seatbelts. The flight attendant came over the speaker and assured us all was well. Right!

It was then I noticed that we were flying *over* Indianapolis. My heart began to pound. Why did the pilot not land? Why? As the flight continued, someone on the other side of the plane exclaimed, "Oh, no! *That* engine is on fire!" Losing one engine was one thing. Losing two, we all knew we were going to be in trouble. The captain's voice announced, "We are having some minor engine problems, but we will be landing shortly on schedule in Evansville."

Trying to conceal her emotions, the flight attendant came by and instructed everyone to put lap trays up and to tuck our heads into our laps to prepare for an emergency landing—just in case. I heard people sniffling. Someone exclaimed, "God, help us." Fear reigned as we descended at a faster speed than normal. Suddenly we thumped and bumped, skidded, and thumped again. As we landed we hit the radar tower, slid off the runway, and stopped six feet from a parking lot. With fire in an engine and foam being sprayed, we jumped out of the plane and ran.

That day fear of the unknown, of having no control and the possibility of facing death, loomed within me. Looking back, I knew I wasn't ready to die. When faced with our own personal tragedy, especially a diagnosis that is life-threatening or disabling, we often react with fear of the unknown. Subtle grief creeps in—grief over the possibility of having to leave our life goals unfinished, or of the ending of our earthly life. Scripture reminds us that no matter what happens to us in the future, God is walking the journey with us.

> *"Do not let your hearts be troubled.*
> *Trust in God; trust also in me."*
> (John 14:1 NCV)

Sometimes There Are No Answers but That's Okay

He was a father, grandfather, and brother who was deeply loved and respected. He always knew how to make people feel welcome and was able to bring laughter into a conversation. Enjoying life on his yacht, when he wasn't at his home, was a favorite pastime. Yes, his life had seen two divorces, and the third marriage was having difficulty. He had experienced some mental illness in his past but for several years had been doing well—or so everyone thought. That was until the call came that this family member had taken his life. There were no words to explain it. All that was left was the pain and grief that accompany such a tragic end to life.

When death comes because another chooses to self-inflict it, the pain and sorrow reach to a place in another's soul that cannot be measured. It is not unusual to feel anger, even while devastated by the loss. There are so many unanswered questions. Those close to the one who committed suicide wonder whether it could have been prevented. They may even feel guilt for something done or left undone. Suicide, as no other form of death, has the ability to disrupt and bring despair to those still living, knowing the death was by choice.

What we know is that God's love is so much bigger than we can fathom. It is God's will that no one should perish. As those who believe in Jesus as Savior, we have been claimed as children of God. The Scriptures assure us that Jesus chooses life for us over death.

Romans 8:1 tells us that there *"is now no condemnation for those who are in Christ Jesus."* Even in suicide God does not abandon His children. My loved one, your loved one, has not been condemned because of the act of desperation he or she may have taken. What a loving God we serve! Find hope in life and live an abundant life, knowing you and your loved one are precious in God's sight.

Paul the apostle wrote,

I am convinced that nothing can ever separate us from God's love. Neither death nor life, neither angels nor demons, neither our fears for today nor our worries about tomorrow—not even the powers of hell can separate us from God's love.
(Romans 8:38–39 NLT)

Desperation and Trust

Four. He was four years old when he was diagnosed with a bacterial disease and put on antibiotics. On this, the tenth and last day of the medicine, he was feeling much better. As usual, I went in to check on him before I went to bed. Something was wrong. Very wrong. I almost didn't recognize my child. His face had swollen until it looked as though it were going to pop. His fingers were enlarged to the point that they looked like a plastic glove inflated with air. I ran from the room and called the doctor. This would not wait until the morning. The doctor instructed me to get him to the children's hospital as soon as possible. "Don't waste any time. I will have a team waiting for him." The forty-minute trip seemed like four hours. As I held my son, who was continuing to swell and was now burning with fever, I prayed. Hard.

Racing into the emergency room with Mark in my arms, I was met by two people in white coats who, without delay, took him and disappeared down the hallway. There I stood, waiting for my husband, who was parking the car. Alone. I wanted to be with Mark. I heard him cry as they took him back. We waited. And waited. Finally, the pediatrician came out and told us that Mark was very sick and that the next few hours would be critical.

Just when we think things are going well, unexpected events can turn our lives upside down. For parents with a sick child, hours agonizingly drag on. For a teen whose friend is seriously injured, or an adult whose loved one is in serious condition, the event sends chills up our spines. We cannot think straight. We cry. We pray. We call others, hoping for some words of hope.

As I sat there beside Mark's bed thanking God for bringing him this far, I heard myself speaking aloud these words: *"Even though I walk through the darkest valley, I will fear no evil, for you are with me" (Psalm 23:4a)*. I knew the doctors had done all they could at that point. Whatever happened, I knew God was right there with us. He loved Mark even more than I did, even though I could not imagine loving anyone more.

Amid life's trials and tragedies there is One in whom we can place our trust, knowing that whatever we face, God knows our desperation and our hopes. Clinging to God each day allows His touch of comfort and strength to be ever present, just as it was for King David when he was hiding and desperate. It was then he wrote these words of trust:

I lie awake at night thinking of you—of how much you have helped me—and how I rejoice through the night beneath the protecting shadow of your wings.
(Psalm 63:6 TLB)

Season Two

Shock Makes Me Stumble

Help! I'm Shocked

Have you ever been zapped by electricity? Maybe you tried to plug in a frayed cord. Perhaps you accidentally inserted a plug into an overloaded socket. Or, you didn't see the need to turn the electricity off for a minor repair (as in the case of my husband who was replacing a light socket in our house). Certain things can send shock waves or electrical currents through our bodies, bringing us pain, burns, or even worse. In that microsecond when the electricity touches our body, our immediate reaction is to retreat. We drop the screwdriver or the frayed cord, or we may quickly pull the plug to disengage the source of the electricity.

How like that brief encounter with physical shock our lives can be when tragedy strikes. Tragedy can zap us and knock our feet right out from under us. It can come unexpectedly and can sear and scar our thoughts and emotions. Whereas the effect from an electrical shock is usually momentary, emotional shock following tragedy can render our lives changed for long seasons of time.

Our son gave us a tree several years ago. It came with no instructions except the notation that it was fast growing. We planted that tree. It grew about a foot, and one day our lawn man ran over it with his lawnmower. The next summer, after it had recovered and once again grown, a tractor rolled over it, breaking its trunk. Talk about shock. This poor tree suffered.

It didn't give up, however. It is now thirty feet tall, and I would say it has withstood abuse no tree should have to endure.

When tragedy comes, in whatever form, our first reaction is shock. I can remember thinking after the tractor broke the tree's trunk, *"That didn't just happen, did it? Well, I guess we will never know what it could have been."* We often cannot fathom things that happen. As with that tree, however, part of our journey from tragedy to joy is our assurance that we carry within us the ability to heal and survive. God planted it there, knowing we would face difficulties. While we don't think of it in this way, grief is a gift. It allows us to heal. Tragedy is not the end of our story because in Christ, we *will* overcome.

"I have told you all this so that you may have peace in me.
Here on earth you will have many trials and sorrows.
But take heart, because I have overcome the world."
(John 16:33 NLT)

Snatching Possibilities

When our family lived in Alaska, we learned that many things grow wonderfully in the cooler temperatures. Decorative cabbage was one of those plants that flourished—as did edible cabbage, peas, cauliflower, and broccoli. We chose to use decorative cabbage in our landscape. As the growing season progressed, our decorative cabbage grew beyond all our expectations. The ruffled, deep purple edges flocked each plant—each a minimum of two feet across. They were *beautiful*. We had plans to enter the largest one in the Alaska State Fair.

One night we heard something outside our window. As we flung open our second-story window and prepared to scare off whatever or whomever it was, our eyes beheld a large moose kneeling, while enjoying the sweetness of our largest cabbage. Nothing we did—banging, yelling, flashing a light downward—deterred this moose from his midnight snack. As the sun allowed us to assess just how much of our beloved plant was gone, we realized that not just one plant, but *every* plant was eaten to just a short stem visible above the ground. Our hopes for the prize ribbon were dashed in an instant, by a source that was interested only in his own needs.

Life is often like that. We have hopes and dreams for a marriage, a child, a career, a retirement—and in a moment they are ripped away from us. There was nothing we could have done to prevent what happened. Still, the disappointment, the sadness (and/or grief) comes like a thief in the night. Sometimes what happens to us cannot be prevented. There is One, however, who knows our pain and promises to give us new hope and a future. As Jeremiah 29:11 assures us,

> *"For I know the plans I have for you," says the LORD.*
> *"They are plans for good and not for disaster,*
> *to give you a future and a hope."*
> (NLT)

When our plans die, God can use our tragedy for His (and our) good.

> *The LORD is close to the brokenhearted*
> *and saves those who are crushed in spirit.*
> (Psalm 34:18)

Natural Disasters

I t was as though the heavens opened all their faucets and let the rains pour down upon us. Living in Georgia, we were used to rain, but this was no ordinary rainstorm. When it finally stopped, roads were cracked, bridges were under water, and homes too numerous to count, were flooded. As I stood with my feet wet from the waters outside, I watched as the water crept ever closer to our home. What does one do when natural disasters threaten all you have?

I stood there, getting even more soaked, hoping and praying that the rising water would not break through our walls. Then I went inside and began to carry things from the the lowest areas to a higher level in the house. Anxiety over the prospect of possible loss from a source over which I had no control swept over me, flooding my emotions.

Ever since that experience, whenever I have heard about floods from hurricanes; devastating tornadoes; fires that consumed thousands of acres of land, including homes; and volcanoes that spewed molten lava over what had once been neighborhoods, my emotions have returned to the flooding in Georgia. While we did not lose our home, as so many recently have, the shock and uncertainty about impending loss are a constant reminder of what life can throw against us—and of what is most important.

In times of tragedy and disaster, it is easy for us to question God. Why didn't God prevent whatever happened? When God created the earth and later humankind, it was completed in perfection. But when sin entered the world, not only humanity but the entire cosmos suffered the consequences. God's design was that a perfect humanity would live in a perfect world. One day we will again see God's perfection. For now, however, we live in a world that is less than perfect. Disasters of all kinds happen. Remembering that God sent Jesus, who died for us on the cross, assures us that God knows and cares about our pain. We may not sense it, but God is always wih us. King David wrote,

> God is our refuge and strength,
> an ever-present help in trouble.
> Therefore, we will not fear, though the earth give way
> and the mountains fall into the heart of the sea,
> though its waters roar and foam
> and the mountains quake with their surging.
> (Psalm 46:1–3)

King David understood that disasters would come, but his source of comfort would always be God. In much the same way, Paul wrote,

> We are hard pressed on every side, but not crushed;
> perplexed, but not in despair; persecuted, but not abandoned;
> struck down, but not destroyed.
> (2 Corinthians 4:8–9)

Whether the destruction comes through fire, wind, lava, water, people doing evil things, or losses that only you understand, there is one source we know holds our future. When we seek God's heart completely, we will find refuge, hope, and comfort.

The Anchor Holds

Sometimes it is hard to find joy when tragedy and disaster come. Grieving is natural. God created us with the ability to grieve. Grief is, in fact, a gift that helps us heal and get through the storms of our lives. But amid the storms, the disasters, and the tragedies, there is One who never lets us go. Calmness often comes after the storm, but knowing God is with us in and through it can help us navigate the rough waters. God wants to be our source of joy amid the storm. God is the One who is our true Anchor.

When I was a teenager, I lived in Niagara Falls, NY. My brother, our friends and I learned to water ski and most summer weekends we could be found on the Niagara River above the Falls, skiing, learning to jump ramps, and doing a variety of tricks in the water on our skis. When we wanted to take a break, we would anchor our boat along the side. While the current of the water was swift, once the anchor was set, we would relax in the boat for a while. The anchor was extremely important. The current was unforgiving and without the anchor, we could have easily drifted too far down river, getting too close to the Falls themselves. The anchor was our source of safety from danger.

When we receive tragic news, our first source of protection from the full impact of what has happened, is shock. It's like the anchor that held us from going to far downstream. Shock helps us process the tragedy in the beginning stages so that when the reality and pain come, we have already absorbed some of the effects. For boaters, it is important to always have an anchor on board. If danger presents itself, it is there to keep you safe.

God is our anchor in all of life. Not only does he lead us through the storms of life, but he is always present with us, like the anchor in the boat. We may feel battered and beaten, but God has told us he is with us-that we will come through our troubled times and that with Him, we can make it through our stormy tragedies. God's anchor holds-always.

When you go through deep waters and great trouble, I will be with you. When you go through rivers of difficulty, you will not drown! When you walk through the fire of oppression, you will not be burned up—the flames will not consume you.
(Isaiah 43:2 TLB)

Stolen

There was only one explanation—and *that* did not seem possible. The seminary I was attending was not in the best part of town, but then again it was not in the worst. Classes were over until after lunch. Rather than carry all my books throughout the day, with the parking close to the buildings, it was easy to exchange books during breaks. Walking to the area where I usually parked, I was confronted by the absence of my car. At first I thought I had forgotten where I had parked. Scanning the lot, it was evident that an empty spot existed where I thought I had parked, but the absence of a car that looked like mine confirmed the uneasy feeling that was surging inside me. My car, with all my books, my purse, my end-term papers—and my Bible—had been stolen. Walking to the empty parking space, my growing anxiety was confirmed. Broken window glass was scattered where I knew none had been before.

I was in shock. My mind whirled. Tears began to well up, and knots filled my stomach. After calling the police and my husband, the only thing I could think to do was to go to my next class. As was customary, we began with prayer. I asked that my car would be found quickly and that my Bible (with all the notes and thoughts I had written next to passages within it) would be recovered. We didn't pray casually that day. We prayed in earnest that wherever had been taken would be found. We prayed in earnest that wherever it had been taken, my car would be found.

Several days later, after we had become convinced that all hope for recovery was lost, the police asked us to identify a car they believed was mine. The owner of the chop shop had called the police! He later said," I knew when I saw the Bible and got in the car that I couldn't work on it. It was like the car had an angel in it or something."

What a story! I was in shock again to find that, even though many things had been taken from the car, my Bible and papers were intact.

As I reflect on the situation now, I recognize that God helped me navigate what I had to do. My shock, my uneasiness, had given way to prayer. It was all I could think to do. Feeling shock after tragedy gives us time to absorb the reality of what we face—and God jumps in to guide us before we ever know it.

"Let him have all your worries and cares, for he is always thinking about you and watching everything that concerns you."
(1 Peter 5:7 TLB)

Numb and Unable to Think

It was a clear day and the Academy students were learning to parachute and free fall from a plane. My husband, being the adventurous and daring person he is, joined with them. Each student had to do five jumps successfully to earn their jump wings. I stood and watched as one after another jumped and landed safely. Because of other obligations, I had to leave after the fourth jumps were completed. Later I learned that on the fifth jump my husband's main riser strap, which attaches the parachute harness to the parachute, had broken. Not only did this momentarily render him unconscious, but it ripped off his helmet and goggles. As he came to, he realized he had to quickly pull the reserve cord, which allowed him to land without being severely injured. However, the cord hit his jaw and ripped past his face, leaving areas of deep bruising. The upward pull after the cord broke caused bruising on his thighs, as well as two broken ribs.

For me as a wife, hearing all of this created immediate shock and anxiety. Sometimes the unknown is worse than the known because our imaginations can go in so many directions. Trying to think the best while at the same time pondering the worst is an aspect of the situation we experience shortly after the news of a serious mishap or tragedy. When the immediate future following an event is unknown, we may remain in shock for days. During those times numbness, functioning on autopilot, and even being unable to think clearly are common. Once the period of shock begins to wear off, the pain of what actually transpired begins to break through, but in the hours, days, or even weeks the shock remains we are able to function—at least minimally.

Like grief, shock is a gift to our minds and bodies. It is God's way of giving us a coping mechanism to get through those first hours or days. It has no timeline and no rules. It's how God created us to deal with the worst of life. To recognize during this season of shock that we are created in the image of God, shows He has provided for our needs and acknowledges that His divine love has gone before us. He knows where we are at and will bring us His gentle comfort, just as a mother bird who covers her chicks with her wings.

Those who live in the shelter of the Most High
will find rest in the shadow of the Almighty.
This I declare about the LORD:
He alone is my refuge, my place of safety;
For he will rescue you from every trap
and protect you from deadly disease.
He will cover you with his feathers.
He will shelter you with his wings.
His faithful promises are your armor and protection.
(Psalm 91:1–4 NLT)

Season Three

Anger Delays Me Reaching My Destination

God, I Am Angry!

I'm angry. You already know that, LORD, because you know everything about me. I have prayed and prayed, but my prayers don't seem to be making any difference. I still feel alone. Am I not good enough to be special? Your Scriptures tell me that you created me, that you love me, and that I am cherished in your eyes. But you don't seem to pay any attention to me. Where are you, God?

Grief and anger. Anger and grief. They often go together and manifest themselves in many ways. Some find it difficult to see God at work in their lives, especially when numerous prayers have been placed before God and He just seems not to be listening. That leaves one to think either that God doesn't care or that one isn't good enough or important enough to warrant his attention. My friend, you are not alone in these insecurities.

In Scripture, David was a man who loved God and wanted to be obedient. At various times, however, he felt abandoned by God. David shared his anger and his loneliness. Because of his circumstances, he didn't know what would happen in the future. He couldn't plan. He had enemies (sometimes our enemies come in the form of anger, depression, fear, anxiety, being enticed by the world that says God doesn't care, etc.) that were constantly wanting to kill him (much as Satan wants to steal and destroy our happiness). He cried out to God to rescue him and told God how he felt. His anger toward God is unmistakable in Psalm 22:

> *My God, my God, why have you abandoned me?*
> *Why are you so far away when I groan for help?*
> *Every day I call to you, my God, but you do not answer.*
> *Every night I lift my voice, but I find no relief.*
> (Psalm 22:1-2 NLT)

Talking to God honestly, sharing your true feelings, helps. David vented his anger appropriately, but he also knew that ultimately, God's design was best, and he trusted amid his anger that God would respond. He ends his rantings with these words:

> *Posterity will serve him;*
> *Future generations will hear about the wonders of the LORD.*
> *His righteous acts will be told to those not yet born.*
> *They will hear about everything he has done.*
> (Psalm 22:30b–31 NLT)

Lemon Pie

Have you ever been so angry that you did something totally irrational? Many years ago, I decided to make a lemon pie from scratch. I had all the ingredients and my mother's recipe, which had stood the test of time—and which created *the best* lemon pie. I put together the crust ingredients: ice water, butter, flour, salt, and vegetable shortening. Something wasn't right. I added a little flour. It still wasn't right. I began to get frustrated. I tried a little more ice water. Tears began to cloud my eyes. And so it went until I was so frustrated and angry that I took the bowl of dough and slammed the bottom of it against the counter. That wasn't enough. I picked it up with a big upward thrust, and the next thing I knew there was piecrust on the ceiling, the counter, the floor—you name it. On top of that I knocked over the flour container. I was angry at myself and angry at the pie dough. Sometimes when we are faced with a tragedy (at the time, my piecrust fiasco felt like a tragedy), nothing makes any sense.

My piecrust was like the tip of the iceberg. At the time I was struggling with mild depression after grieving a loss. No one knew except me. My rage over the piecrust was symbolic of what I felt deep inside. Anger has a way of showing us that something is wrong. If it is a prodigal child, we get angry at her or at someone else who might be leading her in a wrong direction. If it is a loved one who has not cared for himself, we become angry, knowing that things might have been different. If someone else has caused the death or disablement of a loved one (as in the case of a car accident or random evil act), we become enraged at that person. If a spouse was unfaithful, we place blame and direct our wrath at that person.

So many times, when tragedy strikes, anger becomes our focus. Anger at someone or something helps us ignore the pain that is so deep inside. Anger allows our emotions a channel for expression. Anger will however, fester like a blister, until it pops.

The journey through grief is difficult, even for believers. Our strength lies in the reality that we always have hope and God's promises upon which to rely. Even in our anger, God hears the cry of our hearts.

"Understand, therefore, that the LORD your God is indeed God. He is the faithful God who keeps his covenant for a thousand generations and lavishes his unfailing love on those who love him and obey his commands."
(Deuteronomy 7:9 TLB)

Waiting

When I was a child I was told to "just wait" more times than I can remember. It seemed as though I was always in a hurry to get to do the next thing, whatever it was! I can remember waiting for dinner, waiting for cookies to come out of the oven, waiting for friends, waiting for relatives to arrive, waiting to get something special, waiting for my mom to be finished making a dress for me, waiting for Christmas, waiting to be old enough to stay up and welcome in the new year— well, you get the picture. So often we find ourselves waiting. Most common is probably standing in line at the store or waiting for a red light to turn green. Sometimes waiting causes frustration. Sometimes it causes anxiety.

When someone we love has a life-ending illness, waiting and wondering how long before their final day, while still hoping for healing, become the ups and downs of our daily emotional rollercoaster. When my father was dying from cancer, I remember him being so sick, so incapacitated, that he seemed almost lifeless at times. I remember being angry that my dad was suffering so. While I hoped the chemo and radiation would suddenly allow him to return to normal, it was evident that he would soon join others in his eternal home. It was difficult watching him struggle. My heart ached in many ways, but wanting my dad to be out of pain was my heartfelt desire.

My dad somehow knew when his last day on this earth was upon him. The morning of the day he died, he was scheduled to be transferred to a nursing home but told my mother to wait until late in the day. He never left the hospital. Instead, my dad transferred to his eternal home that same day.

For me, knowing that he was no longer in pain brought relief. Yet as the days after his death passed, I began to feel guilty about those feelings of relief. They seemed selfish. My mom no longer had her partner of over fifty years. Searching the Scriptures for peace, I found that these words from Ecclesiastes 3:1–4 (TLB) reminded me that all was well. Dad had completed his journey. It was his time to be welcomed into his eternal reward.

There is a time for everything,
and a season for every activity under the heavens:

a time to be born and a time to die,
a time to plant and a time to uproot,
a time to kill and a time to heal,
a time to tear down and a time to build,
a time to weep and a time to laugh,
a time to mourn and a time to dance.

Like a Volcanic Eruption

He came into my classroom with a reputation for disobedience. The summer before my new students arrived, I wondered what I might do to help this school year be different for him. I prayed for wisdom and about how to engage him, how to show him he was important; most of all, I prayed that God would give me a special heart for this boy.

Finally, the first week of school began. Living up to his reputation, he rebelled against standing in line. He hit more than one student. Within the first several weeks he had gone into other students' desks, broken class crayons, and disobeyed numerous times. What scared me the most, however, was when he took semi-pointed scissors and threw them at another student. This young boy exuded anger at every turn. He was like a volcano always ready to erupt.

I learned that at home he had no rules and did whatever he pleased. He ate whatever and whenever he wanted. I sensed that this child didn't feel loved. He did everything he could to get attention from a parent who was too busy to share life's little moments with him.

When I explained to this child that I wanted to hear about what was important to him, what made him both happy and sad, and that he had been created special, he just looked at me. A few days later, however, he chose to stay after school to help in the classroom. He began to pay better attention and to smile. One day I gave him a note for the principal. It shared how good he had been and how hard he was trying. He returned with a bubbly smile and a special sticker from the principal and gave me a big hug. It was then that the other students started including him, instead of being afraid of him.

Anger has many sources. This child was grieving. All he wanted was to know someone cared. We all have wounds that fester and from time to time send us spiraling. As adults we are good at hiding our anger, but when it comes from a deep wound it sits like grief on our heart. God knows about our wounds and our grief—and our hidden secrets. We may be angry about being treated unfairly, about not measuring up to others' expectations, about not being loved, about being abused or cheated on—and about the loss, in one form or another, of loved ones. God knows our pain just as He knew this young boy's deep hurt, and God's love can conquer even our deepest wounds and grief.

"Don't sin by letting anger control you."
Don't let the sun go down while you are still angry.
(Ephesians 4:26 NLT)

God, Where Are You?

She was only seven years old when she came to live with us. Social Services said she had been brought to their attention by neighbors who saw her digging through trash to find food. She had been left alone with her sister, who was four, and a nine-month-old brother. It was now several days later, and the food supplies in the home had dwindled. She was trying to feed two siblings and herself on scraps.

I will call her Sally. It was evident that the scars from having been abandoned and the previous abuse had taken their toll on her. We tried to show her love and help her connect with her siblings, but it seemed as though we could not reach deeply enough to allay her fears and calm her anger against her mom for leaving.

We took Sally to Sunday school and church regularly. Sally seemed different there, calmer and more relaxed. One day she informed her Sunday school teacher that Jesus had told her to go outside to the trash can to find food. She shared how afraid she had been, because her mom had instructed her not to leave the house or let anyone in. But when Jesus told her to go outside, she did.

Sally's story reminds me of the many passages of Scripture in which people felt totally abandoned. Most, unlike Sally, felt abandoned by God. Today, desertion, rejection, and abandonment remain all too common.

David, Job, Paul—all had times when their anger against God broke out in cries of "Why?" and "Where are you?" David's words in Psalm 13 show just how desperate he was to hear from God. He was angry, believing that God had forgotten all about him. *"How long, LORD? Will you forget me forever?" (Psalm 13:1a).*

From the cross, even Jesus asked, *"My God, my God, why have you forsaken me?" (Matthew 27:46b).* In both situations we know the end of the story. God was there all along. God is always faithful. We know that God's Spirit lives in all believers; therefore, wherever we go, God goes. Because Sally listened to the nudge of Jesus, she and her siblings did not starve, and no further harm came to them. God was moving in Sally's situation, even though she had no way of knowing it.

God goes before us preparing the way; He is our rear guard (Isaiah 58:8), and He walks beside us for our protection (Proverbs 3:26). If you are feeling angry with God because of your situation or a loss that has torn apart your world, know that God is always, *always* watching over you—God loves you too much not to keep watch, because He wants the best for you.

> *The LORD your God goes with you;*
> *he will never leave you nor forsake you.*
> (Deuteronomy 31:6b)

Never Underestimate
a Momma

It was a long, seldom-driven road except during morning and evening work traffic. Those who did drive the road knew the importance of being vigilant for deer and moose. A newly assigned airman to the base was traveling midday and saw a young moose off to her left side. Fascinated, having never before viewed a moose up close, she innocently stopped her new VW bug to watch the baby, unaware that momma moose was watching her from the opposite side of the road. All of a sudden, fearing for her baby's life, the momma attacked the car with the airman in it. When I say "attacked," I mean came down with full force, using her front legs, bumping with her body to the point of totalling the VW. The airman threw herself on the floor of the car, probably preventing her from being physically hurt. When rescuers arrived, she was still crouched on the floor, screaming and shaking. The momma moose, now safe with her baby, wandered further into the wooded area beside the road. This story is true. Its moral: Don't mess with momma!

The airman, after her shock and disbelief, grieved the loss of her new car, which she had purchased only a few weeks earlier. She also became angry at herself for stopping, thinking she should have known better. Anger is one of the emotions that creeps in when harm has occurred through no fault of our own or when we ourselves have harmed another bacause of negligence. That momma displayed rage. Anger in humans, when left unresolved, can develop into rage over things that would never warrant the explosion, if grief were not the cause.

When grief and anger join forces, letting go of the anger allows us to heal more quickly. It also allows God to use that anger to bring love and hope to others who are hurting. God's Spirit can replace our anger with a purpose to better humanity. When we walk in the light of God, He brings us out of the darkness to take His light to others. God does not want us to underestimate the joy we can have when we rid ourselves of our anger.

James, the brother of Jesus, wrote,

Understand this, my dear brothers and sisters: You must all be quick to listen, slow to speak, and slow to get angry.
Human anger does not produce the righteousness God desires.
(James 1:19–20 NLT)

Season Four

Unpredictable Emotions Take Me on Many Detours

Like the Waves
of the Sea

I stood in the water, mindlessly gazing toward the horizon, unaware of an unusually large wave heading toward me. Within seconds I found myself knocked down by the force of the wave. My body fought to overcome the force that pulled me under. As though responding to my fear, the wave flowed backward, more gently, but still powerfully, until it returned to the vast ocean from which it had arisen. I felt my feet touch the sand, and as quickly as I had gone down I stood up and pushed through the water toward the safety of the shore.

As I stood a safe distance from the next waves coming in, I realized that what had taken place was a metaphor for the journey through grief many, including myself, face. What once seemed like an ordinary day was interrupted by news that hit like the wave that had just knocked me down. We flounder, try to stand strong, but find there are times we just cannot. Then slowly the sting of pain begins to lessen, like the receding waters, and we once again begin to regain our balance.

Three years after my brother died on what had been his birthday, I was standing at the kitchen sink fixing dinner when, like a large wave that could not be contained, the tears began to flow. They had been bottled up within me as I had tried for so long to stand strong. Memories of times we had

Photo by Pexels.com

spent together growing up rushed back like an unstoppable tsunami. I missed my childhood pal and teenage confidant. I wanted to celebrate another birthday with him.

Grief is never complete. Life moves on, but like the constant ebb and flow of tide-driven waves, within the hearts of those who grieve there is a place that is forever fluid. Our normal day gets disrupted by a sight or smell or sound, and suddenly we are transported to a place of sadness and remembering. Some days our emotions hold sweet memories, like the gentle ripple of the tide that touches our toes. Other days the intensity of grief may cause the simplest of tasks to overwhelm us.

Even though the journey in grief changes, God never does. He understands the fluctuation of our emotions. When the waves of the Sea of Galilee terrified the disciples, Jesus spoke and all became still—including the fear within the disciples. The psalmist confirms that God heals the brokenhearted (Psalm 147:3) and tells us to cast our burdens on the Lord, assuring us that God will sustain us (Psalm 55:22). That is the Good News, comfort, and strength in which we can rest as the waves come and go in our journey through grief—because we *can* do all things through the One who gives us strength (Philippians 4:13).

Switchbacks

Shortly after we moved to Colorado, I decided I wanted to climb Pike's Peak. Not having tackled anything like that before, I sought wisdom from some who had. The advice? Get in shape, train, hike, train—you get the picture. So, I formed a group of hikers with the goal to climb Pike's Peak at the end of the summer. Weekend hikes of increasing length became the norm. Finally, the day we had all been training for arrived. Pike's Peak is locally called a fourteener, meaning that it is over 14,000 feet in elevation—14,110', to be exact. We made reservations at Barr Camp (elevation 10,200') for the first night—a very welcome site after the day's endeavor—before continuing to the top the next day.

The hike began with what are known as switchbacks, 13 of which mark the beginning of the trail. The best way to describe a switchback is like a letter *W* on its side, repeated many times. To an inexperienced hiker like myself, these switchbacks were a little daunting—and they were just the beginning of the trek!

Since that hike I have often thought about those switchbacks. Throughout the climb there are those steeper areas of switchbacks, followed by a mile or so of gentler hiking. Along the way one will see beautiful scenery, unique rock formations, wildlife, and more switchbacks leading to an

ever upward destination, until one reaches Barr Camp. During those rough times along the trail there were signs signaling our progress. The most encouraging one was the marker that tantalized us with only "one mile to Barr Camp"!

How like life that hike was! We have times of smooth going, and then those grueling switchbacks come—times when it appears we are getting nowhere, when the climb seems so hard that we wonder whether we will make it. Then things seem to smooth out again for a while. If I had given up during those first 13 switchbacks, I would never have experienced the beauty amid the struggles along the way, nor the joy of reaching Barr Camp, the destination for that day.

As I was hiking, I kept repeating over and over again words from Paul (*I press on toward the goal. I press on toward the goal.*)

*Forgetting what is behind and straining toward what is ahead,
I press on toward the goal to win the prize for which God has
called me heavenward in Christ Jesus.*
(Philippians 3:13b–14)

Jesus said,

*"Here on earth you will have many trials and sorrows.
But take heart, because I have overcome the world."*
(John 16:33 NLT)

In grief we take one step at a time, knowing God will help
us reach His goal.

Attacked

Walking the mile home from school was a daily routine. What wasn't routine was what took place this particular day. On this day, our after-school band practice had finished, but because I was the drum majorette I stayed after practice to clarify some details with the band director. Because it was Fall, the summer's growth of wild grasses along the pathway was at its peak. About halfway along the path, something didn't feel right. I turned to see a tall, older teen about fifty feet behind me. I wondered from where he had come, as I hadn't realized anyone else was on the path. Then I noticed that he was increasingly walking faster, narrowing the distance between us. An uneasiness settled upon me as I also picked up my pace. I remember thinking, *He has longer legs and is probably just walking fast to get home.* It was then that I felt his long, muscular arm around me and found myself being flung into the tall grass. While screaming, I tried to wrestle my way free. His strength was too much for me, and the knife he pointed at me held all the power he needed. I remember thinking, *God, help!*

After I eventually found my way home, my parents quickly called the police. The knife was still in the grass, but there were no leads to identify the person who had changed forever my levels of trust and vigilance. I knew life was not fair. I knew bad things happened. But they weren't supposed to happen to *me*!

Some life events change us forever. The memory of that attack haunted me for years. I became angry. Why would someone want to do this to *me*? Did this person think he had a reason? Did he even know who I was? I was angry at myself for not running when I might have had the chance. Why didn't I protect myself? God, *why*?

As I tried to put my life back together, there were times when I cried, times when I exploded for no reason, and times when I just wanted to be left alone. One day my youth leader reminded me that Scripture says it rains on the just and the unjust. She also gave me a piece of paper with *Proverbs 15:3* written on it:

> *The eyes of the LORD are everywhere, keeping watch on the wicked and the good.*

While it didn't change my situation, the passage allowed me to recognize that God saw it. The attacker didn't, in the long run, get away with what he did. I also realized what a fantastic, life-giving verse I had received. When we doubt God's love for us, when we wonder where God is, or when we think God is too busy for us, the truth is that He is keeping watch.

Play Ball!

The umpire called, "*Play ball,*" and with that the game began. Expectations were high for those of us rooting for the home team. We were having the best season in years. Championship was within our grasp. First inning: 2–0. That was okay. We would catch them and win. Second, third, fourth innings: 5–1. Could we do it? Bases were loaded; we could come close. Fly ball, third out. Fifth, sixth, seventh innings. The pattern continued. Instead of cheers, groans could be heard from the home team stands. The eighth inning came—score? 8–4. With the eighth inning final out and the time getting late, people began to make their way out of the stands, disappointed.

Have you ever given up on something? Has life disappointed you? Have you asked, *Why me?*

Top of the ninth, resigned to a home team loss, A hit! Runner on first. Another hit. Runners on first and third. Another hit. Two home, one runner on second. One out. Another hit, runners on first and third. The faithful observers stood and cheered. At bat was a player who had struck out twice before. Shouts abound. *C-r-r-rack!* The home run exceeded all expectations. What a game. What a rollercoaster of emotions.

We have a friend who has a child with Down's Syndrome. When most couples learn they are to become parents, they have hopes for a perfectly normal child and envision what that child might accomplish in his or her lifetime. As the months go by and new life is felt, expectations and excitement grow. Then an ultrasound reveals that there is a problem. Further testing and measuring of the baby inform the couple that, in fact, their child will be born with Down's Syndrome. While happy for the new life within, disappointment, questioning, guilt, and grief over lost hopes—a variety of fluctuating emotions come and go. This was not what they were hoping for, but they would persevere and do the best they knew how. Nine months of waiting, and their special child was born.

Fast-forward six years. This child with Down's is now playing softball on a special team. She can do most everything (in her own unique way), and she has brought so much joy and laughter to her family. Yes, there have been surgeries and struggles. But perseverance and love have shown this child, and her parents, that she is very special.

Life can throw us curve balls. We will experience struggles. Sometimes there will be no apparent answers. We will grieve losses of many kinds. Feeling the pain, facing the realities, forgiving ourselves and others, and seeing life through the lens of our final inning on earth can bring joy out of sadness.

Those who sow with tears
will reap with songs of joy.
(Psalm 126:5)

Fear

Fear. That's what I felt when I was a small girl and first stood close to the edge of the water tumbling over Niagara Falls. Back then, not all the heavy railings had been installed that now instill in visitors a feeling of security. I remember fearing that I could fall into the raging torrents of water and be swept right over the precipice, crashing onto the rocks below. I remember holding tightly to my mother's hand while we both felt the mist created by the power of the water cascading over the rocks. I remember wanting to back away to a place where, in my mind, both my mother and I would be safe.

Older now, I have returned to the falls several times. Even with the sturdy railings providing more protection, I cannot shake the sensation of being swept away, of crashing down upon the rocks, of being sucked into the whirlpool beyond.

There is a part of the grief journey that is like standing at the edge of the falls and wondering whether we might be swept away. When we lose a loved one, especially a spouse, our sense of security seems to crumble. There are times when we feel as though we have been hurled against the rocks, only to be further swept into a torrent of unending tears, anger, and fear of the unknown, wondering whether we will survive. Sometimes we are not even sure we want to survive because we no longer have that secure hand onto which we can cling. Like the mist that dampens those who experience the power

of the raging water, tears for those who grieve remind us of the loved one now gone from our own lives.

And yet, when I stand amidst the mighty thunderous waters, I cannot shake the wonder of it all. The same God who created this marvel created me with a yearning to connect to Him. Just as He does the birds of the field, God cares profoundly about my needs. God's Spirit in me longs to afford comfort. His love for me wants to provide peace.

Whatever season you may be traveling through in your journey of grief, if you can picture God providing all you will need to bring peace in the future, the prospects will not be so fearful. As when the sun shines on the mist of the falls and a rainbow appears, God's promises of His care are forever.

"So, don't be anxious about tomorrow. God will take care of
your tomorrow too. Live one day at a time."
(Matthew 6:34 TLB)

Just a One-Flight Jump

If you have ever raised or been around children, you probably have encountered some with enthusiastic curiosity and a frightening lack of fear. When those two qualities combine, life can quickly get very interesting. Our family had returned from a camping trip, and our children had deposited their sleeping bags at the foot of the stairs that led down to our front door. Apparently the sight of numerous fluffy, rolled up sleeping bags presented our third son with a great idea. Not taking time to fully examine the possible danger, he catapulted himself from the top step onto those sleeping bags. This would have been a great idea—except for the sideglass of the door, which was directly behind those sleeping bags.

Most any parent, hearing a loud crash and shattering glass and knowing there are children in the house, would probably have the same reaction I did. Panic! Running to the front door, I found James, lying on top of the sleeping bags with glass all around him. I didn't see any blood, which was a good sign. When he flashed his boyish grin at me, I took that as another one. After I had gotten him away from the glass and made sure he was not hurt, other emotions quickly took over. *"What were you thinking? Didn't you see the glass? Haven't we told you not to jump on the stairs?"* I think you get the picture.

What a vast variety of emotions we experience in our lifetimes. Grief can call up emotions we didn't realize existed in us. There are shock, sadness, guilt, irratibility, rage, despair, regret, anxiety, loneliness, denial, resentment, yearning, worry, isolation, self-pity, fear, hopelessness, and too many others to write. The point is that grief leaves no part of us untouched. Additionally, we don't experience these feelings one at a time, in any semblance of order. They come and go, cross over, find places to hide until an opportune moment, and are unpredictable.

Even years after a tragedy something may bring back a memory and call forth emotions we had thought were gone. As with the glass we fixed, emotions have a purpose. The glass gave our home protection, just as our emotions provide an outlet for feeling and processing our grief. Allow yourself to feel. Share your emotions with a trusted friend and know you are getting stronger, as you recognize that the emotions are a reflection of something or someone you continue to hold very special in your heart.

> *Trust in the LORD with all your heart*
> *and lean not on your own understanding;*
> *in all your ways submit to him,*
> *and he will make your paths straight.*
> (Proverbs 3:5–6)

Unspoken Fear

A small child, an older boy, a young teen. Throughout his life he had seen his father come and go. As a young child, he didn't understand why daddy was gone for so long. "When is Daddy coming home?" Weeks and months crossed off on a calendar were a help but didn't bring much comfort. As an older boy, he anticipated the times of separation, but it was still hard to see his dad pack his suitcases. As a teen, understanding his dad was being sent overseas and that countries were fighting where he was going brought a sense of fear, but he usually kept that fear to himself. At night he and his mom would pray for his dad to be safe and to come home soon, but until he saw his dad come through the door each time, the fear remained.

For military children and adults, knowing that a parent or loved one lives in harms way every day and night, there is a fear and grief about the unknown that seems ever-present. Daily life goes on, but in the quiet times, especially at night, the darkness sometimes speaks loudly, things you do not want to think.

As someone who has experienced extended periods of separation from her spouse and watched her children grieve the absence of their father, there are times when all I could pray was, "God, watch over him. Protect him." But I also knew tragedy could come, and in some ways, the children had to be prepared.

Living in hope, living each day knowing that whatever happened, even if death came, it would not win because my spouse believed in Jesus Christ as Savior, brought me strength to help the kids know that just as their dad was praying for them from wherever he was, if he went to heaven, he would pray for them from there—and that one day they would see him again. More importantly, however, we learned to trust as a family. John 14 became my mantra many nights. Jesus wanted his disciples to have peace, no matter how dreadful things looked. He wanted them not to fear. He doesn't want us to fear. As The Living Bible says, "I am leaving you with a gift—a peace of mind and heart!"

Those words helped to calm a young boy's and a teen's heart—and they helped us through those rough days of separation.

"I am leaving you with a gift—peace of mind and heart!
And the peace I give isn't fragile like the peace the world gives.
So, don't be troubled or afraid."
(John 14:27)

Depression Causes Me to Go Back

The Great Cloud

A brother who was murdered. A son who died in a car accident. A dad who died of cancer and a mother whose heart just gave out. A brother-in-law who committed suicide, a dear friend who died much too early from a heart attack, a mother-in-law who died shortly after heart surgery, and a father-in-law who suffered Alzheimer's before his journey on this earth ended. These are just a few of my loved ones who have become part of the great cloud of witnesses talked about in Hebrews 12:1–2a (see below).

There is no question about it. When someone dies whom we have dearly loved, there is a place within us that will never again feel the same. Many would say that a hole has been left in their hearts.

Even regarding those who die in Christ, their death brings an earthly sadness that sometimes makes us feel as though we are in a desert, alone. But there is a blessing that sometimes we fail to remember—a blessing that can bring our saddened hearts comfort and joy. Before Jesus died and thus overcame death on our behalf, death had held the victory. But through His sacrifice the battle with sin and death was once-for-all-time won! Our loved ones who have made the transition have gained all that Jesus prepared for them. They have experienced the unwrapping of a gift that we cannot yet imagine.

When we truly trust that Jesus does what He says He will do, we know our loved one is no longer struggling. Rather, the one we love is at perfect peace. Is there anything better than that?

Knowing that life beyond death is a believer's hope, we who are still on this earth can celebrate *with our loved one.* We can also know that whatever pain we may now feel is temporary. Amid our daily struggles, we can cherish the joy in which our loved one now lives, and in which we will one day take part.

Therefore, since we are surrounded by such a great cloud of witnesses, let us throw off everything that hinders and the sin that so easily entangles. And let us run with perseverance the race marked out for us, fixing our eyes on Jesus, the pioneer and perfecter of faith. For the joy set before him he endured the cross, scorning its shame, and sat down at the right hand of the throne of God. Consider him who endured such opposition from sinners, so that you will not grow weary and lose heart.
(Hebrews 12:1–3)

Precious Tears

Have you ever stopped to consider that God is keeping track of all your sorrows? Not a tear falls that goes unnoticed. God has been present every step of your life and mine. He knows the heartaches we have endured. As we have called upon God in our darkest times, as tears have cascaded down our cheeks, in His great compassion God has taken notice.

As David recorded in *Psalm 56:8,*

> *You [God] keep track of all my sorrows.*
> *You have collected all my tears in your bottle.*
> *You have recorded each one in your book.*
> (NLT)

What a magnificent image of God's love for us! While being hunted down by Saul, David was running from place to place trying to hide. Desperate for his life, he cried out from the depths of his soul, through tears, to God—the only One who could transform his future from impending death to life. His trust in God's faithfulness and care gave him hope.

Most all of us have shed tears over a situation that seemed hopeless. I know I have. There have been tears of grief, tears of frustration, and tears because of betrayal, to mention a few. Yet, thinking about God being so intimately involved in my life (and yours) that He can catch tears reminds me of just how close God is all the time. We are never away from His presence. God knows each of us intimately, and our tears are important to Him—so important, in fact, that He keeps track of them. God always has our back! (Now, *that* is awesome!)

Life challenges us. One day everything seems fine, and the next we have a mountain of misery to climb. When this happens, tears often well up and overflow, stinging our eyes. Like David, we can trust God's love and imagine our tears being caught by God in His special bottle. The tears are no longer ours but are being touched by God's heart of compassion. What comfort it is to know that God, who is as close as our heartbeat, who understands our pain, is walking with us on our journey and is always at work on our behalf, to turn our mourning into dancing and our grief into joy!

God collects my tears in His bottle and writes them in His book. One day He will redeem everything I have been through. My story will end well.

A Tug-of-War

When I was a little girl, one of the highlights of every summer was our family reunion. I loved those reunions because they were the only times I got to see all my aunts, uncles, and cousins together. We usually had a softball game or some other activity that got almost everyone involved. One of the things we kids liked to do was a tug-of-war. Looking back, I don't know why it was always boys against girls, because the boys won almost every time.

As I remember those times playing tug-of-war, I realize that my journey through grief has been like that game. In the middle of my grief was a deep, dark cloud of sadness and depression. Pulling on one side was the strength I was receiving, knowing in my head that God was with me. On the other side, however, were some who told me it was time to let go of the past and move on. This side of the struggle called up feelings of inadequacy for facing the future. There were doubts, fears and a multitude of other negative thoughts about myself. Often there were days when I was not sure who would win the tug-of-war.

One day someone asked me where I put my trust. It took me back to the tug-of-war. The boys won most of the time because they had someone on the end of the rope who knew how to remain steady, and who would not give up—someone who could be like a rock, immovable and solid. Even if we get tired and let go in life, there is still One who doesn't. That One is God, who not only keeps faithful watch over us but gives us power to overcome our struggles and keep on keeping on.

Have you never heard?
Have you never understood?
The Lord is the everlasting God,
the Creator of all the earth.
He never grows weak or weary.
No one can measure the depths of his understanding.
He gives power to the weak
and strength to the powerless.
Even youths will become weak and tired,
and young men will fall in exhaustion.
But those who trust in the Lord will find new strength.
They will soar high on wings like eagles.
They will run and not grow weary.
They will walk and not faint.
(Isaiah 40:28–31 NLT)

God's Whispered Plan

I have a plaque that is hung in a place where I see it several times a day. The words on the plaque read "Be silent that you may hear the whisper of God." Each time I pass by that plaque my mind and my heart seem to join, and I find myself repeating "Be still and know that I am God."

These words are like gold to me—a gift every time I read them. In 1 Kings, there is a wonderful encounter between Elijah and God. God finds Elijah hiding and speaks to him:

"Go out and stand before me on the mountain," the Lord told him. And as Elijah stood there, the Lord passed by, and a mighty windstorm hit the mountain. It was such a terrible blast that the rocks were torn loose, but the Lord was not in the wind. After the wind there was an earthquake, but the Lord was not in the earthquake. And after the earthquake there was a fire, but the Lord was not in the fire. And after the fire there was the sound of a gentle whisper. When Elijah heard it, he wrapped his face in his cloak and went out and stood at the entrance of the cave.
(1 Kings 19:11–14 NLT).

So many disasters and so much violence seem to be happening in our world. Bad things happen to innocent people. We get frightened. We hear unwanted words. Life is not what we had expected or hoped for. Some are quick to blame God for not preventing whatever has happened that has caused them grief. Sometimes we think we cannot go on, that we cannot face another day—and like Elijah we run and hide. Trying to cope the best way we know how, we retreat within ourselves.

What Elijah found when he listened for the still, small voice (familiar KJV language from 1 Kings 19:12) of God is that God had a plan to give Elijah a future. Like Elijah, when we listen for the whisper of God and allow our hearts to stay focused on the One who breathes life into our souls, God's voice stills the rumbling in our minds, the shivers that move through us, the charring that burns our hearts and steals our joy and peace. God desires to renew our troubled Spirit and refresh our souls. Elijah found that, rather than darkness, fear, and death, God wanted to breathe new life into His prophet. That's what God wants to do for us, no matter what has happened in our lives that causes us to want to run.

Peace in the Darkness

When I was little I used to have terrible nightmares. They would awaken me, and I would be so scared I couldn't even find my voice. To venture downstairs in the dark to my parent's room, was not an option! So, knowing they would hear the "thud," I would purposefully "fall" out of bed and land as loudly as possible! Soon I would hear my mother coming up the stairs. She would gently touch me and help me back into bed, sit beside me softly talking—reassuring me that all was well and helping me fall back to sleep. I knew everything was okay because I knew Mom was there, but there was more: Mom carried within her God's presence. I saw her pray, often on her knees, beside her bed. Mom brought Jesus with her into my room.

Throughout the Scriptures God told His followers not to be afraid. Even facing unbelievable odds, Moses passed on to Joshua these words:

> *"Be strong and courageous! Do not be afraid and do not panic before them. For the Lord your God will personally go ahead of you. He will never fail you nor abandon you."*
> (Deuteronomy 31:6)

The angel Gabriel told young Mary, "*Do not be afraid . . . you have found favor with God*" (*Luke 1:30*). And Jesus assured His disciples that He would be with them until the end of the age, telling them not to be afraid (Matthew 28:20). Over and over, no matter the task, the message of Scripture is that we are not to fear: God is with us.

When, because of tragedy, we find ourselves feeling very alone, fearful of living our lives in the absence of a spouse or child or friend, the message is that God is right beside us. Not only that, but the cloud of witnesses (including our loved ones) is rooting for us, saying "You can do this!" (Hebrews 12:1).

God's Spirit comforts us in times of trouble; guides us through the unknown; speaks to our hearts in that still, small voice (in the familiar parlance of the KJV rendering of 1 Kings 19:12); and desires for us to rest in His peace, knowing He is *always* with us—we are never alone. Even if we cannot feel God's presence, He is still always watching over us.

Psalm 34:18 affirms that the Lord is close to the brokenhearted. Jesus himself said,

> "*Peace I leave with you; my peace I give you . . .*
> *Do not let your hearts be troubled and do not be afraid.*"
> (John 14:27)

Tomatoes and Compost

Having a compost bin has become popular among home gardners over the past decade or so, so when we moved and planted a garden we joined forces with those who compost. Last spring we noticed several tomato plants growing out of compost that had wintered over in a large bin. Jokingly, we allowed those plants to grow, expecting them to eventually die. The joke was on us, however, as those tomato plants grew and grew; because they had extremely fertile soil from which to draw nutrients, they far surpassed any of our regularly planted tomato plants. We wondered whether the tomatoes would taste any different, and so, with expectation, we picked the first compost tomato when it was ripe. It was one of the sweetest and juicest tomatoes I had ever tasted, much better than what I remember from those grown in the garden the previous year.

That compost tomato plant spoke to me about times of depression and doubt in my life. There were times when a tragedy or loss had occurred that all I wanted was the familiar—what I knew. I wanted my life to be back to normal, my old friends to be nearby, to walk into my parents' house and see them sitting in their chairs, or to see our son's impish smile and share a hug with him. I could not move forward because I was tightly clinging to the past—even though I knew things could not return to the way they had been.

It's not that what I had experienced in my past wasn't good enough. It absolutely was. But what I saw in the compost plant was that God could take what I no longer had and create something that would give me hope and life once again. That tomato plant represented my ability to survive harsh times, times of being tossed about or with other people making life difficult. Even the way I thought about my life was less than useful at times. The compost tomato was a symbol that life would go on and could once again be good. When placed in the Master Gardener's hand, our grief and the struggles of the past can be rebirthed as something beautiful.

"I waited patiently for God to help me; then he listened and heard my cry. He lifted me out of the pit of despair, out from the bog and the mire, and set my feet on a hard, firm path, and steadied me as I walked along. He has given me a new song to sing, of praises to our God"
(Psalm 40:1-3a TLB).

Season Six

Forgiveness Helps Me Breathe Fresh Air Along the Way

An Unexpected Response

How does one begin to understand the evil that exists in the world? Yes, we know that sin pervades our world and that humanity has been given free choice, but still—when that evil makes a direct strike on a loved one, how do we begin to cope? How do we let go and allow God to make things right in His way?

The day after we learned of my brother's murder, we packed everything in our van, leaving behind what was to have been a fantastic vacation with friends and our children at Disney World. The children occupied themselves, knowing it would be a long journey from Florida to Kentucky. The only sounds that could be heard were my deep breaths, trying to conceal the sadness that overflowed from my eyes. That was until our seven-year-old son declared, "Mommy, I will get whoever murdered Uncle Ken if it takes forever."

My heart, already torn into pieces, felt as though arrows had just shattered it more. Did I want the person who took my only sibling to face the consequences? Absolutely. Did I want our son to focus on what it would take to accomplish this? Absolutely not. I knew that revenge bred hatred and resulted in a hardened heart. In that moment I had a decision to make: how to respond to our son, who saw his mother in so much pain.

I turned to him, looked into his deep brown eyes, and said, "David, what the person who murdered my brother did was wrong, very wrong. But *we* don't want to do something that is wrong too. Right now, the only thing I know to do is to pray for him. Maybe whomever it is doesn't know Jesus. We can pray for him to know Jesus, can't we? David, Mommy needs to pray that I can forgive the person, too. Do you want to pray with me that we can both forgive whoever it was?" We prayed. To this day I am not sure how I was able to say those words, but something was transformed in me as we prayed for the murderer and for us to be able to forgive him. Many more prayers were offered about being able to completely forgive. But at that moment, God took a tiny piece of the wrong that had been done and replaced it with a peace that began the healing process.

God wants our whole heart. When we allow even small pieces to remain in our own control, we cannot experience the fullness of God's peace and joy. If we remember that God's plan for us is to be filled to overflowing with what He wants, then letting go of the pieces that harm us just seems right.

"For my thoughts are not your thoughts,
neither are your ways my ways,"
declares the LORD.
"As the heavens are higher than the earth,
so are my ways higher than your ways
and my thoughts than your thoughts."
(Isaiah 55:8–9)

I Wonder . . .

I wonder. Many years ago, I worked with another minister who would regularly preface her time of staff devotions with "I wonder . . ." Then she would continue to ask some pointed questions like, "I wonder how the woman at the well felt when Jesus told her all the things she had done. I wonder how she felt when Jesus forgave her of her sins, which she knew were many."

Sometimes it is hard to forgive. When someone ignores advice and their poor choices cause them chronic illness and/or death, we can feel angry. While we grieve the loss of their health and/or their death, we at the same time, may find it difficult to forgive them for putting us through the pain and sorrow we feel. We might pause to speculate, *I wonder if she knew how much she was hurting me by not listening. I wonder if she didn't care enough about me to stop hurting herself? Was I not important enough or loved enough for her to want to stay well?*

When I told coworkers that God was calling me to leave my current profession and become a full-time minister, there were several on the staff who spread rumors and talked about me in ways that brought me to tears. To this day I do not understand why this happened. Sometimes I just wanted to confront the people and make them admit their lies. One day, however, as I was reading in Matthew, these words jumped out at me:

Then Peter came to Jesus and asked, "Lord, how many times
shall I forgive my brother or sister who sins against me?
Up to seven times?"
Jesus answered, "I tell you, not seven times,
but seventy-seven times."
(Matthew 18:21–22)

Ouch. I wanted justice, but God's Word reminded me that *I was guilty* for not forgiving them. Jesus had forgiven *me* more than seventy-seven times (or however many times I had sinned). I knew what I had to do. I can tell you that it wasn't easy because I had to see these people every day. But God changed my heart when I chose to forgive and to see each person as His beloved—even if it meant I had to forgive what I thought was nearly unforgivable.

Make allowance for each other's faults and forgive anyone
who offends you. Remember, the Lord forgave you,
so you owe it to others to forgive them
(Colossians 3:13 NLT).

Fleas and Forgiveness

He was a tiny, farm-born kitten and the one that came home with us to be our pet. He had only one problem— F.L.E.A.S. Our adorable kitten had not just one or two fleas. He was covered from being born outside and living in the field with his mother and siblings. The fleas had to go. We brought our little guy inside and proceeded to give him a little bath, hoping the water and flea shampoo would wash them away. We did the best we could, dried him off—and discovered that some of the fleas were determined to stick around. It took several baths, flea shampoo, and later flea powder to eradicate all those fleas that had taken up residence on our kitten.

There have been times in my life when someone has done something to me that "ate" at me; made me angry; kept me focused on their lies or negative physical actions; and, in essence, took away my joy. I don't know about you, but when someone hurts me, especially intentionally, or doesn't care if I get hurt emotionally, they become like one of those fleas. They bother me. What they've done bothers me. I try to forget what they did, but their actions just keep biting away at my inner peace.

It's time to take a bath. Forgiving someone is like getting a bath—and sometimes we need more than one bath to get completely clean! We try to forgive whomever caused us pain or sorrow, but what she has done keeps coming back in our mind. When it does it usually comes with anger or hatred or a feeling of unforgiveness.

The good news is that once those fleas were gone, that little kitten didn't itch anymore. He could sleep peacefully and purred contentedly. We knew he hadn't liked his baths, but getting rid of what was hurtful made a better life for him. Forgiveness is the same. To find peace and inner joy, we must forgive. From the cross Jesus asked His Father to forgive the ones who had not listened, who had hurt and mocked Him, and who had condemned Him to death. Forgiving someone sets us free to be who we were created to be in Christ—to be washed white as a field of newfallen snow.

> *Sprinkle me with hyssop, then I will be clean.*
> *Wash me, then I will be whiter than snow.*
> *Let me hear you say, "Your sins are forgiven."*
> *That will bring me joy and gladness.*
> (Psalm 51:7–8 TLB)

Forgive Myself?

The cars each had one teenage girl in them. One was on her way home from local college classes. The other was on her way to work. Both were known in the community, from loving families, and well liked. Their lives were forever changed in an instant when, for reasons unknown, one of the girls did not see the other car turning onto the road and broadsided her on the driver's side. The girl in the car that was hit lingered for several days but did not survive.

The young girl who had caused the accident was injured, but not severely. She told her mother that she wanted to attend the funeral of the girl whom she had hit. When she arrived at the funeral home, she seemed to be okay. The moment she stepped into the receiving room, however, she became weak; began to sob uncontrollably; and, with the help of others, was taken to another room. As a pastor, I tried to help her in her grief. At one point she sobbed, "How can I ever forgive myself? I killed her."

There are times when we feel as though what we have done cannot or should not be forgiven. That is what this surviving teen felt. She could not forgive herself, knowing what she had done. Those whose grief finds no peace can take comfort in the reality that God feels and knows our pain. He understands the terrible grief and guilt we hold in our heart. God's love for us is so deep that He has already provided a way for us to find His peace and joy again. It begins with realizing that Jesus died *for you*. His death on the cross was just as much for you as for any other person.

The apostle Paul (then Saul) hunted down and killed those who were believers in Jesus as Savior. Later, after Saul had encountered the risen Christ and sought God's forgiveness, God used Paul powerfully to spread the message of salvation. Paul had to seek God's forgiveness and also forgive himself so that he could let go of the past and become the individual God had created him to be. Forgiving requires courage and strength. When we forgive ourselves, God can bring a Spirit of wholeness and hope as He fills us with joy and enables us to follow His path for our life. We honor Jesus on the cross when we forgive both others and ourselves. Forgiveness opens the way for each of us to make a difference in the lives of others.

One thing I do: Forgetting what is behind and straining toward what is ahead, I press on toward the goal to win the prize for which God has called me heavenward in Christ Jesus.
(Philippians 3:13b–14)

Seeing Beyond the Tree

The place where I first heard this was on the television, during a commercial. As with many commercials, the sponsor or the reason for its airing did not leave an impression. However, the message came through loud and clear: "God promised that everything will be okay in the end. So, if everything is not okay, then this is not the end."

What a profound, yet simple, truth. Sometimes I think I cannot see the forest because of the tree right in front of me. Tragedy and loss of any kind have a way of focusing our attention on that one thing. We become consumed with what has happened and cannot grasp that there is a bigger picture into which God will place our situation.

When Paul was ministering and spreading the message of Jesus Christ, he faced all types of trouble. He was run out of towns, stoned, imprisoned, and beaten. He was shipwrecked, bitten by a snake, sick and close to death, lonely, disowned by many fellow Jewish people, and seemingly forgotten at times. But Paul never gave up. He saw a bigger picture than the difficulty facing him at any particular time. Here's what he wrote:

We are pressed on every side by troubles, but not crushed and broken. We are perplexed because we don't know why things happen as they do, but we don't give up and quit. We are hunted down, but God never abandons us. We get knocked down, but we get up again and keep going.
(2 Corinthians 4:8–9 TLB)

So, we do not look at what we can see right now, the troubles all around us, but we look forward to the joys in heaven which we have not yet seen. The troubles will soon be over, but the joys to come will last forever.
(2 Corinthians 4:18 TLB)

I think that Paul's trust in what Jesus taught, and his knowledge of how God had been faithful to those who loved Him from the beginning of time, permeated all of Paul's thinking. There wasn't a doubt in Paul's mind that things would be okay in the end. God said so, His track record said so, and He had always kept His promises. While Paul did not make popular the saying that caught my attention, he surely could have. Truly, if everything is not okay, then this is not the end.

If I try, I think I can see the forest more clearly now. The vista before me has so much collective beauty. If I listen, I can hear the birds singing, small critters scampering, and the wind rustling the leaves.

"Don't let your hearts be troubled. Trust in God, and trust also in me."
(John 14:1 NLT)

Oh, for a Bath

Being a military family meant that we moved frequently. One of those moves was from Louisiana to Alaska in 1980. It was definitely a big move, especially back then when there were no cell phones, and the land lines had several-second delays in sending spoken words to and from the Lower 48.

We packed up our Minnie Winnie RV with as much as we could, knowing it would be a long trip with three young boys to keep occupied. After making our way north, stopping to see some special sights and visiting with family along the way, we crossed over into Canada. We met the Alaska Canadian Highway in Dawson Creek, British Columbia. Back then only about 400 of the nearly 1,400 miles were paved. The rest of the road was rock and gravel—and mud, if it rained. Because of the road conditions, sometimes rutty and with holes to avoid, the average speed was about forty miles per hour. While all of this may seem unreal, it was an exciting trip that we will never forget.

Remember, I said the road was muddy if it rained. It did. It rained more than one day. The mud from the road covered our RV. The mud was joined by bugs and dust from the road on sunny days. If we had not known the Minnie Winnie was cream colored, we would have guessed shades of dark and medium brown, with dirt clumps clinging onto the rear bumper.

What does all of this have to do with our journeys in grief? As we traveled we accumulated more and more dirt, until we could hardly decipher the original design on our RV anymore. When we encounter a tragedy or loss, there are times when, because of pain and/or guilt, we blame someone or something else. It always seems easier to live with blaming than with forgiving. What happens, though, is that each time we don't forgive it's as though more clods of mud stick to our bumper. They didn't fall off because of the bumps in the road. They had to be s.c.r.u.b.b.e.d off—and it wasn't easy. Forgiveness usually isn't.

When we finally hosed down the RV, scrubbed it, hosed it again, kicked off some of the clods that clung tightly, and hosed it again, our Minnie Winnie was like a new RV. She had a fresh, new look, and because of all the weight that had been washed off, not just from her outside but from inside the engine compartment as well, she ran much better. She had accumulated so much it had been compromising her performance.

When we forgive, whether it is someone who is guilty for our pain, or ourselves for choices we made or didn't make, things we said or didn't say, God's Spirit in us cleans us up from the inside out—and we are truly transformed with God's love.

"Be kind to each other, tenderhearted, forgiving one another,
just as God through Christ has forgiven you."
(Ephesians 4:32 TLB)

Season Seven

Acceptance Helps Me See the Clouds Moving On

C.H.A.N.G.E.

When computers first became the new thing, I must be honest and say that I resisted. I liked pen and paper. I liked sitting with books in front of me doing research. I just didn't see how computers could really change my life that much.

C.H.A.N.G.E. For some it comes easily. For others, like myself, trying to keep up with our ever-changing world sometimes causes frustration and anxiety. However, there are times when, if I don't move forward in my thinking and learning, I feel as though I'm surrounded by cobwebs.

Life is full of change. We can either choose to embrace it or push as hard as possible against it, dig in our heels, and become prisoners to the past. I think that adapting to change—at least for those of us who are inherently change averse—requires courage. It also involves faith in God for what lies ahead because most often we cannot see the future clearly. Sometimes we may catch a glimpse, but for it to become clear we must step into it. Once I decided I *might* want a computer, I began watching other people who were using them. I began to see possibilities I had been missing, staying in my pen and pencil, book-in-hand world.

Taking that first step wasn't easy. Actually, it was scary. As recorded in Joshua 3:14–17, the Israelites had a big decision to make. The only thing standing between them and their promised home was the Jordan River, at flood stage, probably about ten feet deep. To cross the river, they would have to trust God. Note in verses 15–16 that, *before* God would stop the water's flow, the priests would have to dip their toes *into the river*:

As soon as the priests who carried the ark reached the Jordan and their feet touched the water's edge, the water from upstream stopped flowing.

In grief, when we reach a point at which we no longer cling tightly to the past but entertain possibilities concerning the future, we have reached a true turning point. Grief teaches us. As we struggle and conquer the next thing (whatever that might be), we discover inner strength. Sometimes we are not ready to move on. It's okay to languish for a season, until we are ready to acknowledge the strength God puts within us to not only survive but to survive well, and to live out God's promises of hope and a future for us.

As we think about new possibilities, we know that God has already been wherever it is He is asking us to go and has prepared the pathway for us. That means that, even if we doubt or find the situation scary, God will provide what we need. Yes. We can do what otherwise might have seemed impossible because God is with us with every step.

What Was I Thinking?

What was I thinking? It was three in the morning and I couldn't sleep. Often when I have a night like that I read a book. On this night, however, I woke up and thought, *I'll hang that picture in the kitchen.* I got my hammer, a nail and the picture; moved a sturdy, solid oak dining room chair into the kitchen; and proceeded to get up onto the chair and reach over the tall pantry to hang the picture. All was just fine—until one leg on the chair gave way. Not having anything to break my fall, I went tumbling down. On the way, I hit the front of my head on the sharp corner of the counter, which flung me into the doorframe, on which I hit the back of my head. Unable as I was to find my balance and still in motion, the crazy angle of the chair on which I had been standing caused me to lunge forward again, hitting my head on the counter a second time and propelling me backward over the chair into the doorframe, finally allowing me to crumble onto the chair itself, which was now lying sideways between the counter and the doorframe.

After regaining consciousness, I realized I was now bleeding from a long cut on my leg and feeling intense pain in my head. *What was I thinking?* I'm not sure! There are times when things we do cause us to suffer the consequences for some time to come—in some cases permanently. Why was I determined to hang the picture at three in the morning when no one was around to help? Why did I choose to stand on a chair instead of a stool? Why did I make my way back to the bedroom and lie down and go back to sleep? *What was I thinking?*

The result of my picture-hanging fiasco was a traumatic brain injury that adversely affected my short-term memory and has resulted in long-term life adjustments that have brought frustration and tears at times, knowing as I do that some of the things I used to be able to do I no longer can.

Some of you may be facing loss of memory or other health issues that force a new normal in your life. After accepting that my memory would always be compromised, I conceded, "Okay, God, what's plan B? What am I to do now?" God wants to take our circumstances and use them for good. Even from a hospital bed, the light of Christ can shine as encouragement to others. Life may be different, but God brings hope when we feel hopeless.

> *My body and my mind may become weak,*
> *but God is my strength.*
> *He is mine forever.*
> (Psalm 73:26 NCV)

God's Perfect Home

Four years ago we were looking for a retirement home. We searched and searched the web and had a realtor sending listings. We went through some that seemed to be possibilities. Finding the right home was not been an easy experience. It did, however, teach us a great lesson.

During the search, several houses were located that could have been a good choice. They had most of the features we wanted, and we made appointments to go through them. House #1: the morning of the appointment the realtor called and said it had gone under contract the night before. House #2: the same thing. House #3: for several days I could not connect with the seller (it was a for sale by owner), so I drove by the house and found her outside. I talked to her and she informed me, "It went under contract last night."

Oh, I forgot to mention that for weeks before my search began I had fervently prayed that God would not allow us to purchase just any home but *the* home God desired most for us. I prayed even if I thought a particular prospect was perfect, asking that God would close the door on it if there was another location, another home that would open doors for God's kingdom. So when those houses went under contract just before I was to look at them, I trusted. After the third house went under contract, I knew that God was actively participating in our house hunting process.

And then, when I saw it, when I walked in the door, I knew. I knew it was the one. There wasn't a question. We went under contract, and the process went smoothly on the home that is now ours. That's the short version of the story—but there is really so much more.

Throughout our search I kept being reminded that God already has the perfect home prepared for each one of us—that there is no "contract pending" unless we have not accepted Jesus as Lord and Savior. The door to our new home is open, whenever the time comes for us to "move."

Whether we are young or old or in-between, for believers the best is always yet to come. We can celebrate our lives in this temporary world while looking forward to the glorious eternal life with no sadness, no tears, and no pain.

> *For this world is not our home; we are looking*
> *forward to our everlasting home in heaven.*
> (Hebrews 13:14 TLB)

Standing in
the Doorway

The sight is forever etched in my mind. Standing at the end of our driveway, a neighbor and I were chatting, briefly connecting as we checked for mail. Suddenly the ground beneath us began to shake. I could see the car rock and feel my heart pound, knowing that my children were inside the house that already showed evidence of the earthquake. I ran, wanting desperately to rescue my children. Then, through the cracked picture window, I saw them—three boys standing beneath the archway between the living and dining room, just as we had practiced during earthquake drills. Our oldest was holding his sister, one was standing straight and tall like a soldier, and the other had a smile on his face as he waved at me. They had followed the plan; all was well. It could, however, have turned out much differently.

We never know when tragedy will strike, but when it does we often find ourselves reeling from it and trying to make sense of it. The book of Ruth is a wonderful story of the ups-and-downs of life. It begins well. Naomi and her husband have two sons, and even though they feel compelled to emigrate to Moab because of famine, they settle in their new home and their sons marry. Then Naomi's husband and two sons all die, leaving three widows in a time when widows usually became destitute. Naomi decides to go back home. Her daughter-in-law Ruth goes with her and makes her home with Naomi, who cannot see anything good about her situation. She even wants to change her name to Mara,

because the Almighty has made my life very sad. When I left, I had all I wanted, but now, the LORD has brought me home with nothing. Why should you call me Naomi when the LORD has spoken against me and the Almighty has given me so much trouble?
(Ruth 1:20–21 NCV).

In her deep grief Naomi blamed God for her trouble. Blaming God or someone else for tragedy allows us to deflect our pain and make some "sense" of our situation. Naomi could not see any future for either Ruth or herself.

Bad things happen, but God works on our behalf to restore life to us—life that trusts in God's love and provision. God guided Ruth and eventually Ruth married. Naomi later became a grandmother—her most cherished wish at this juncture of her life. When we are grieving, there are times when we, like Naomi, want to give up. We feel hopeless and cannot see any possibilities for future happiness. God wants us to be hopeful, to stand strong with Him, and to trust Him. If that is all we do, it is enough for God to see us through.

"For I know the plans I have for you," declares the LORD,
"plans to prosper you and not to harm you,
plans to give you hope and a future."
(Jeremiah 29:11)

Surviving the Storm

Among the oldest trees on the earth, growing where few other things can survive, twisting against the strong mountainous winds, the Bristlecone Pine Tree lives on Mt. Evans in Colorado, along with a few places in California. Regardless of the incessant winds, thin, dry soil, and winter temperatures that rarely rise above freezing, the Bristlecone Pine gives evidence of how it has adapted to its location at over 11,000 feet in elevation.

I first saw a lone Bristlecone Pine at a distance when I rode the cog railway up Pikes Peak. It was then I learned about them and discovered that these very specimens had already been living when Jesus walked this earth. I decided I wanted to see and know how these trees withstood such adversity.

These rare trees have learned to survive by growing slowly, often adding only 1/100th of an inch in girth each summer and not adding any ring to their trunks during droughts. While most trees replace their needles each year, bristlecones conserve energy by using the same needles for decades at a time.

There are times when tragedy or loss has entered our lives that we cannot fathom moving forward. There are struggles in abundance, details that must be attended to, and often bereaved family members who themselves have needs, not to mention our own raw emotions and desperate attempts to hold life together.

Photo by Chao Yen/Flickr

This rare tree holds lessons for us who grieve. First, it allows itself to adapt rather than break. When severe winds threaten it, rather than bending and breaking it allows itself to twist with the wind, giving strength to its trunk. As we give ourselves permission to change and believe there will be a future for ourselves, we become stronger. When the environment gets rough, the tree slows down, conserving its resources. It gets moisture from the dew in summer and the snow in winter, again using what it can to remain faithful to what it is—a tree. Sometimes we may think we are going to break under the pressures we face. Grief takes time. It comes and goes, like the weather conditions on the mountaintop. But like the dew that nourishes it, God supplies His living water, His Spirit within us, to sustain us and help us remain strong when we rest in Him and His abundant love.

> *[God] said to me, "My grace is sufficient for you,*
> *for my power is made perfect in weakness."*
> (2 Corinthians 12:9)

The Master Fixer-Upper

Recently there have been several shows on TV about people buying a "fixer upper" house. On these shows, after the house is purchased, a professional examines the walls, the flooring, the roof, the electrical, the foundation, the plumbing, the HVAC system (heating and cooling)— you name it, they check out everything. In the process they often find hidden issues they weren't expecting. Sometimes there are leaks in the walls. At other times the foundation is cracked or sagging. They discover hidden problems like mold, asbestos, lead pipes, carpenter ants, termites, and structural issues that could bring disaster.

To the rescue comes the professional, who can, sometimes creatively, fix the problems. In the end the house turns out sturdy and transformed from what it formerly was. With tears of joy, attempting to express their gratitude in words the new owners cannot seem to find, the painful experience and the weeks needed for the transformation fade into soon to be forgotten memories. An opportunity for new memories to be made pushes the struggles permanently into the past.

God is our Master Fixer Upper!

No matter what the world has thrown against us, no matter if what happened has been the worst thing imaginable, even if there is no way we can envision ourselves living normally again, like the professional who may need to get creative to fix a disaster, God will take our messes and use them to not only help us find new possibilities in life, but to show us how to reach out and use our messes to help others. Where we think there is no way, God will show us His way.

Our Master Fixer Upper (Jesus) has experienced whatever it is that has torn us apart—even things too unthinkable to mention. Loss, rejection, betrayal, and death are well known to Him. He has, after all, been through *the valley of the shadow of death (Psalm 23:4b NKJV)*. Not only has He been through it—He has triumphed over it all!

When people purchase a "fixer upper" and hire a professional to make it the best it can be, they make the choice to put their trust in that person. None of us is alone in having places that need the touch of our Master Fixer Upper. Trusting God and allowing Him to make us spiritually and emotionally whole is the best makeover ever.

What, then, shall we say in response to these things?
If God is for us, who can be against us? He who did not spare
his own Son, but gave him up for us all—how will he not also,
along with him, graciously give us all things?
(Romans 8:31–32)

Lydia

Her name was Lydia. Years ago, she was a student in my classroom. The impact she had on me has remained to this day. Her small frame was topped with thin, very light blonde hair that usually looked as though she had tried to do something special with it but, as a seven-year-old, could not figure out how it should be. Lydia was one of those students who was liked, but one of the last chosen because she didn't seem to excel at anything. One day during our sharing time she showed a picture of her sister. She briefly described her, telling her name and age, and then one of the other students asked why her sister was in a special chair. Lydia's smile faded, and quietly she responded, "My sister is dying. She can't walk anymore. She can't hug me like she used to. I wish she could."

Tears welled up in her eyes. A holy hush fell upon the room. I motioned for Lydia to come to me, but on her way another student stood up and, as though directed by God, hugged her with a childlike bear hug. Then another joined the hug, and then another.

Lydia's sharing allowed our class to join with her in her struggle, which before she had carried in silence. The death of Lydia's sister brought grief for our class. Lydia's faith, however, brought comfort to us all. A few weeks after her sister's death, Lydia stood up during our sharing time and announced, "My sister is with Jesus, and *guess what*? She doesn't have any more tubes, and she can walk and run and smile, and when I die we can hug each other again!" Lydia had a huge smile on her face as she talked about what heaven was like for her sister. Her faith and trust in the promises of Jesus allowed our class to heal along with her.

With her childlike faith, Lydia taught us that when we share our grief, our burden seems lighter. She taught us that, even in death, loved ones touch our hearts in ways that can never be diminished. Most of all, Lydia taught us that no matter our size or the way in which the world sees us, God's Spirit in us brings comfort beyond understanding.

Whoever dwells in the shelter of the Most High
will rest in the shadow of the Almighty.
I will say of the LORD, "He is my refuge and my fortress,
my God, in whom I trust."
(Psalm 91:1–2)

Hope and a New Normal Show Me the Path More Clearly

Moving Forward:
Being a Blessing

Twelve. Over the course of my life, I have called twelve states home. Living in many places has been a rich blessing. However, I learned quickly that if I was going to fit in—or understand what others were talking about—I would have to learn the local lingo, the "isms" of the language.

One of the first terms I learned after moving to Alaska was *termination dust*. Originally, it signified the ending of seasonal jobs in the mines. More recently, however, the term has come to refer to the first few snowfalls that appear on the mountaintops—usually beginning with a dusting visible from miles away, signaling the impending termination of the summer.

While many parts of the "Lower 48" have dazzling sweeps of color that signify the changing of the season, Alaska has one prominent autumn color—golden yellow. Fall is brief and intense. The trees turn gold and yellow while the snow creeps ever lower on the slopes above the towns. Each day the snow migrates farther down the mountain, until one morning there's a white winter wonderland all around.

Winters in Alaska can be very harsh if one is not prepared. I have thought about the warning the termination dust gives to those who pay attention. Winter coats, hats, gloves, and boots are once again placed within easy reach. Snow shovels and bags of Ice Melt are brought from storage areas. Car owners

make sure their engine heaters are ready to be plugged in and an emergency food supply and water are tucked in the trunks. When one lives in Alaska, one gets prepared for what is to come!

Termination dust reminds me of so many stories recorded in Scripture in which Jesus warned folks to be prepared. Jesus specifically talked about how we are to be prepared for His return; we will not know when it will happen, but there will be warning signs for the vigilant.

Finding a new normal in our lives after traveling the difficult road of grief gives us the opportunity to help others see the beauty that can once again come. Our "keeping watch" can be found in the manner in which we live our daily lives. As we draw near to God, we can hear God's purpose for us more clearly. As I have pondered this time of "keeping watch," I think words of John Wesley speak loudly and clearly: "Do all the good you can, by all the means you can, in all the places you can, to all the people you can, as long as you ever can." While our past as we knew it is gone, our future holds the beauty of what God can do through us in this time of preparation."

"Be dressed ready for service and keep your lamps burning."
(Luke 12:35)

Fog!

On the top of the Appalachian Mountains in Pennsylvania there is a retreat center where I attended a conference. To say the view from atop the mountain was breathtaking would be an understatement! The autumn leaves provided a kaleidoscope of colors—colors that changed daily right before my eyes, from green to yellow or gold orange or burnt orange or red or deep burgundy. Leaves, caught by the wind, floated in the air, often combining with others to create a small "tornado," only to be caught by another whoosh of wind and carried elsewhere.

One day I was taking pictures when the fog began to roll in on the mountaintop. I had taken a picture of the trees, admiring their myriad of colors, and only minutes later those same trees were partially hidden, their colors clouded, and their vivid presence easily missed.

There are times in our journey through grief when fog is all we can see. Nothing seems clear. Some days we don't even want to get out of bed. The nights seem longer because of the darkness that surrounds our hearts. There are days when our minds are overwhelmed, and we are unable to see our way clearly. Just as the fog eventually concealed the trees from my view, when we are in the middle of a season of fog we cannot catch a clear vision of anything. Life has no ostensible purpose. But God's Spirit within us is never dark; it is always Light. God's light offers a clearer vision for our lives than what we could

ever see on our own. It can reveal the myriad of opportunities awaiting us as we trust in God for our days and weeks ahead. We may not yet be able to see a new future clearly, but when we allow ourselves to be guided by God, we are assured that all will turn out well.

> *Where can I go from your Spirit?*
> *Where can I flee from your presence?*
> *If I go up to the heavens, you are there;*
> *if I make my bed in the depths, you are there.*
> *If I rise on the wings of the dawn,*
> *if I settle on the far side of the sea,*
> *even there your hand will guide me,*
> *your right hand will hold me fast.*
> *If I say, "Surely the darkness will hide me*
> *and the light become night around me,"*
> *even the darkness will not be dark to you;*
> *the night will shine like the day,*
> *for darkness is as light to you.*
> (Psalm 139:7–12)

A Master Design

Both my grandmothers and my mother enjoyed quilting. One year I decided to take a quilting class with visions of how beautiful my own quilt would be. As I worked on blocks that were to become a wall hanging (we started off small), I often pondered how very much like quilts our lives can be. We begin our lives whole. But just as the fabric gets cut into strips and squares, we too, bit by bit, strip by strip, become fractured and broken—no longer complete. At times we may feel like a pile of scraps, at other times like pieces needing to be put back together. As I sewed the strips, squares, and triangles together, I began to see the scraps combine to become beautiful pieces— not the same as when they had been whole, but in some ways even more striking because of the love and care that had gone into making sure they were right.

One day as I sat at the sewing machine, I realized that because God knew the pain and sadness I had experienced, if I let Him have all the pieces of my messy life, He could take those bits and pieces and form something beautiful out of them. I had tried. I had cried, shopped excessively, ignored warning signs of depression, hidden my sadness, and so much more. But as I began to sew Jesus into the manger on my wall hanging, all I could think about was that Jesus left His home, suffered, and died for me. Those pieces that formed the face of Jesus did more than occupy a special place on my creation.

They cut deeply into my soul. Jesus wanted to put *me* back together. I knew God wanted all my pain. I didn't have to hold on to any little bit.

The more we allow God to put our pieces together in the way He desires, the more peace and joy become woven into our days. God is in the piecing and mending business. While our new life may not look the same as it once did, it can become a new and equally beautiful creation from God. Just as we cannot see how a quilt will look until the last square or triangle is sewn into place, neither can we visualize in advance all the plans God has for us. When we begin to create something like a quilt, we have faith that it will turn out well. God is our Master Designer. He knows just what is needed to put our broken lives back together.

The heavens are telling the glory of God;
they are a marvelous display of his craftsmanship.
Day and night they keep on telling about God.
(Psalm 19:1–2 TLB)

Something New

While I was on a vacation, a skilled basket weaver taught me his craft. After arriving at his studio, I was instructed to pick out the types of reeds, their colors, and any additions I wanted to create my own unique basket. Because this was going to be my "one of a kind" creation, I carefully selected what I thought would go together nicely. Then my lesson began.

I learned how to secure the reeds to the bottom, giving the basket a sturdy foundation. Then, carefully weaving, I learned to tap each row against the previous one. This tapping was needed to give the basket strength after the reeds dried. The craftsman taught me how necessary it was to regularly turn the spindle on which I had placed the basket, so that it would get an even shape. Along the way, the colored reeds were woven in, giving it my own personal design. Finally, I was ready to finish the uppermost reed, securing it by tucking and weaving it into the previously woven reed.

When I was finished, the artisan directed, "Now turn it over and sign your name, and put the date on it." WOW! This basket had *my* name on it. It made me think about how God had put His inscription on each of us when we accepted Jesus as our Savior. His imprint is also etched on your beloved in eternity, claiming him or her as His own.

When I first began to weave my basket, I had an idea of what it might look like, but until it was finished it was only an idea. Sometimes it was difficult to get the basket woven just right. I made some mistakes that had to be corrected before

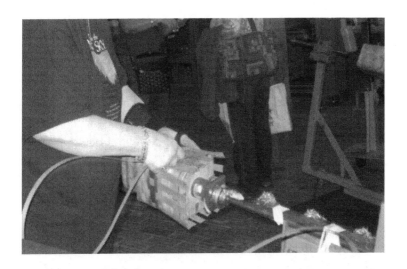

going on. I have thought about how God wants to weave our lives, with the beautiful memories of our past, into something only He can perfectly complete.

We are God's creation! His fingerprint is inscribed on our hearts and on our futures. God's master plan takes our past—including our mistakes and sorrows—and weaves it into our futures, incorporating possibilities only He can know in advance.

After we lose a loved one or some other tragedy touches our lives, our vision of our future is altered. But just as the artisan's hand was always there to guide me, God's Spirit within us guides us as we find and settle in to our new normal, based on God's eternal purpose for our lives.

As *Psalm 139:13-14* reminds us,

> *For you [God] created my inmost being;*
> *you knit me together in my mother's womb.*
> *I praise you because I am fearfully and wonderfully made;*
> *your works are wonderful,*
> *I know that full well.*

Trusting the Journey

This painting by John Lorenz has spoken to my heart so many times. For me, the fence represents not only my faith journey but also the way grief has moved in my life. Things may be going smoothly; all is well, as one might say. Then tragedy strikes. It may be the loss of someone we love, the termination of a job, a move that forces us to leave behind dear friends or family, or a myriad of other unwanted situations. No one escapes some sort of tragedy or loss—they are intrinsic to life.

When tragedy or loss come, we often find ourselves heading in different directions from what we had planned. As we look ahead, things that were once very clear become faded and at times almost unseen. There are decisions we must make as to which way we will go. We find ourselves facing emotions we never thought we would experience. We vacillate between wanting to see hope and thinking there is no hope. Some days the sun seems to shine, and other days the storm looms heavily upon us, causing us to feel lethargic or depressed. We may feel lost with no direction in which to go.

Grief has its seasons. Most of the emotions and our daily struggles are normal following a tragedy that has changed what was once routine. One of the things I notice in this painting is how the tree is encircled by light, a light that seems to extend into the distance. While grieving, the pathway to a new normal

may seem clouded and almost invisible or impossible to follow. But God's light shines even in the darkest of corners. God's love and light will guide us to places He knows are best for our future—when we are still, and trust in Him. The words on the painting quote *Psalm 46:10a*, *"Be still and know that I am God."*

Later, in one of his talks, Jesus said to the people, "I am the Light of the world. So if you follow me, you won't be stumbling through the darkness, for living light will flood your path."
(John 8:12 TLB)

A Lesson from
Two Moose

Have you ever been late for something? I have, more times than I care to admit. On one occasion however, I had the best excuse ever. Living in Alaska, we were on our way to church—or so we thought. With four children ready to go, I opened the door, and there stood two moose in the driveway. If you know anything about moose, you know that you cannot just say "go away" and expect them to listen! The moose noted our presence by turning their heads but were not in the least impressed that we might need to get to church on time. We had a standoff. The moose won (I did after all, know better than to argue with a moose!). About 15 minutes later, after the moose had chewed on some plants and I suppose were bored, they finally left—and we got into the car with a great story to tell as to why we were late for church. It is a great story, isn't it?!

For some reason I have been thinking about events that changed the way I deal with life. Whether or not the two moose knew it, they impacted my spiritual thinking. Rather than getting totally frustrated over being late, I decided to enjoy watching the moose from a safe, but close distance. As I studied them, I realized just how disproportional their heads seemed to be to the girth of their skinny legs. The size of their nostrils—well, actually their snouts—seemed enormous. Even now, as I recall studying those two moose, I remember thinking just how uniquely God has made each species—and each one of us!

What I understood that day was that if I make decisions to "breathe in" all the wonderful moments that surround me and let go of some of the things that distract me, I will experience "God-moments"—brief gifts of God's abundant grace flowing through "the ordinary" moments in my day. That encounter with the moose has blessed me over and over as I have learned to just relax and allow God to open my eyes and ears to His abundant gifts all around me. Healing from tragedy and grief takes time. Like the moose in the driveway, it cannot be rushed. In that time when we begin to see through eyes of wonder, moments of joy will find us.

Every good and perfect gift is from above,
coming down from the Father of the heavenly lights,
who does not change like shifting shadows.
(James 1:17)

The Dance

We gathered each week with anticipation. I remember anticipating the opportunity to learn to dance. I also remember anticipating the awkwardness of being paired up with a partner who might be cute, or was possibly a great dancer—or then again might be one of the less than ordinary guys who were there under protest and who generally had two left feet. Looking back, I am sure I fell into the latter category, as the boys also came with varying degrees of anticipation.

Many in the class already had great rhythm, knew how to be suave, and made an impact with others who were similar. For those of us whose rhythm didn't seem to connect with their feet, there was a struggle to look cool and give off the aura of knowing what we were doing. I remember the looks the boys would give when partnered with particulary popular girls—and their expressions when paired with those who were less than popular.

Our dance instructor was there to teach us the Waltz, the Fox Trot, the Tango, the Jitterbug, and the Cha-Cha-Cha. Popular dances back then had strange names. Some were known as the Mashed Potato, the Pony, the Twist, the Bump, and the Chicken. If we did well, paid attention, and didn't waste time, the last ten minutes were a reward during which we could express our abilities with these newer, strange dances.

Grief has a way of making us feel as though we don't fit in. If we used to be part of a couple and now are single, it's awkward being with other couples. The same is true if our circle of friends was based on work, a location, a hobby, or some other shared activity or interest. After loss we see life differently. Living in grief has its way of separating us also. Not only do we feel sad, joyless, or hopeless, but others may tend to avoid us, wanting to share life with those who make them feel happy.

Our church hymnal contains a hymn titled "Lord of the Dance" written by Sydney Carter. Every time I hear this hymn, my mind recalls those dancing lessons, the emotions expended in trying to look as though I knew what I was doing, and sometimes feeling awkward and insecure about fitting in.

One Sunday, I read the words of the hymn intently. They described the life of Jesus, using the metaphor of a dance. His life had so many times of disappointment and loss. It also included times of overcoming. It was on that Sunday morning, reading those words as though for the first time, that new possibilities flooded my heart. God knew how I felt. He wanted me to dance joyfully and find the new possibilities He had for me as I trusted Him to be my partner, navigating the days ahead. *That* is what God wants for each of us!

Weeping may last through the night,
but joy comes with the morning.
(Psalm 30:5b NLT)

Praises and Thoughts

Clouds of Praise

It happened about halfway between Kentucky and North Carolina on one of those long stretches of highway where it seemed there was not another car on the road except mine. Throughout the drive I had been aware of the clouds that signaled rain ahead. But at this moment, as I gazed up at the clouds all around me in the sky, I could see layer upon layer—from fluffy white to heavily laden gray, from whispy to broad expanses, the sky looked as though it went on forever. It was the type of sky that, to a child lying in the grass, was captivating. And then, a song, "The Face of Love," played on the radio. I had not heard it for several years, and the words went straight to my soul: "*I have seen the face of love, the grace of God, the face of love.*" The lyrics went on to talk about how once the heart had yearned and feared that all it held would remain silent . . . but then . . . again those words—"*I have seen the face of love, the grace of God.*" It took me by surprise; Jewel spoke the words of my heart.

My gaze began to penetrate even more deeply into the clouds, to observe how all the different layers and types of clouds seemed to express so much of what we each hold inside—so many longings, so many hopes, things that oftentimes only God knows. But wasn't that precisely the message: that *God knows.*

The words went on: "*So take my hand and all I know; with it I also give my heart. If God were a flame, I'd allow myself to be consumed and if God were the wind, I'd wish for God to pass through me, because I have seen the face of love— the grace of God.*"

I have indeed seen the face of love, love that came as a baby in a barn manger; love that grew and helped us understand just how much God loves each one of us; love that, no matter what, is always with us. In those moments I journeyed from the cradle to the cross to the crown of my Lord, and my heart was so full of God's love for me, and for you, that all I could do was sing and weep, because I had seen God's face of love. I have seen it in pain and sorrow. I have seen it in the difficult times of change and trust. I have seen it in the joy of accepting that God has a plan not only despite, but even through the pain, and of seeing God's love take me to places in my life I might never otherwise have ventured to go.

In their silence the clouds drew me in to remind me that in this world, where darkness sometimes seems to be so invasive, the hope of the One who loves us so much, is that others would also see the face of God—the grace of God in you and in me—because the light of Christ in us is brighter than any darkness.

May God's love transform your mourning into deep, lasting joy.

"The joy of the Lord is my strength"
Janet

Index of Feelings